My Polish Grandmother: from Tragedy in Poland to her Rose Garden in America

By Stephen Szabados

DEDICATION

To my grandmother, Anna Chmielewska, we miss you.

Table of Contents

INTRODUCTION

This book is about my Polish grandmother. After World War I, she immigrated from the Russian partition of Poland. *How did her experience differ from the men's?* I wrote this story of her life, hoping to offer a different perspective on Polish immigration by telling it from a woman's perspective, which is different from most immigration stories. Therefore, I tried to uncover the differences by asking the following questions:

- *What challenges and fears did the Polish women overcome when they left home to establish a new life in a new land?*
- *What were their fears when they left their comfort zone around their village and family?*
- *Did they travel with a friend, or were they alone?*
- *Were they excited when they saw electric lighting and indoor plumbing for the first time in the cities and on board the ships?*
- *How did their experience on the ship differ from the men's?*
- *Why did a male family member have to be at the port before officials admitted the women?*
- *What were their visions of America?*
- *How did their vision differ from men's?*
- *What made finding a husband so crucial for her?*
- *How did they adapt from farm life to urban life?*

This book describes my grandmother's birthplace, early life, and the events that shaped her before she left for America. The story tells of the challenges she overcame when she traveled across the Atlantic to the United States and found herself alone in her new country. The story ends by describing her new life in America and, hopefully, shows how she found the strength to build it.

I wanted to go beyond the photo albums' names, dates, and pictures in writing my grandmother's story. I hope describing the events of her life will show a different perspective on Polish immigration to America. It is crucial to ask why she did what she did.

My grandmother, Anna Chmielewska, was the youngest of nine children and the smallest member of the Chmielewski household in Poland. As an adult, she stood under five feet tall and weighed less than 90 pounds. However, she was in charge of her house in America. My grandmother quietly dominated her home. My parents, sister, and I lived with my grandparents for about ten years. We all did things her way. She did not have a dominating personality but commanded the room without demanding. She never raised her voice. I would describe her as a kind and loving person, but I think the family followed her instructions because they loved her, not out of fear of her. She was a tremendous inspiration in my life.

After researching her family history, I believe she gained inner strength from the tragedies of her early life in Poland and the challenges she overcame to start her new life in America.

Her father died when she was still an infant, and she grew up on a small farm in Poland, where everyone in the family had to work every day to survive. Her parents had nine children: three daughters and six sons. However, four of the boys died as toddlers. Surviving was not easy.

Everyday life was hard when Anna grew up in Poland, but it became terrifying during the summers and winters of 1915. Her mother, Julianna, died in April 1915. Then, the violence of World War I destroyed many farms in the area as the Russian Army retreated through the area using a scorched earth method to delay the Germans. Homelessness, hunger, typhus, and cholera descended on the area, and the Chmielewski family experienced these tragedies. I often asked Grandma what happened to her and her family during the war. She would not talk about her life. Her only comment was, "We survived!"

The rebuilding began after the war ended, but Anna no longer belonged on the Chmielewski farm. Her parents were dead, and her brother had inherited the farm. Her sister-in-law was now in charge of the Chmielewski household. Her brother Boleslaw was busy rebuilding the farm, but he was also responsible for finding Anna a husband. As the married head of the family, Boleslaw needed to find a Polish husband of "noble birth" for his twenty-year-old sister. It was time for her to leave the family home.

Boleslaw could not find his sister a suitable husband among the surviving Polish men. Boleslaw contacted his brother Hipolit in America to resolve this problem and ask for his help. They decided to send Anna to America and have Hipolit help her find a husband there. Again, finding a suitable husband in Camden, New Jersey, was difficult. Finally, after two years, her brother arranged a marriage with the cousin of one of Hipolit's Polish friends. This step was still a considerable challenge for Anna, since he lived 900 miles from Camden, and she met him for the first time a week before the wedding, when she got off the train in Bloomington, Illinois.

In America, Anna worked hard every day. She worked as a maid at a hotel, in a hospital laundry, and as a cook at a neighborhood restaurant. Anna also cooked and cleaned for her family every day. However, she still found time to be happy, working in her garden and spending time with her family.

Why are the stories of our ancestors important? They were simple people. However, they are more than names, dates, and places on a chart. More importantly, their lives made significant contributions to our lives. They played an essential role in our family history. We must capture the family stories that will bring our immigrant ancestors to life for our children and grandchildren.

Our ancestors were part of the wave of emigration that left Europe in search of work and a better life. It was not easy to immigrate to

America. They saw immigration to America as their last chance. They had to overcome obstacles, travel from their village to the ships, and endure hardships as they crossed the Atlantic. Then immigration officials required them to prove they were worthy of admission to the United States. Once here, they faced challenges and discrimination in finding work and improving the lives they sought.

This book asks questions about Anna's fears about making these changes. How did she face these fears? How did she overcome them? Although I found no answers, I gained new insights into my grandmother.

As you read Anna's story, ask the same questions about your ancestors. If you do, your view of your family history will change. Hopefully, you will find insights to help you understand your immigrant ancestors.

My grandmother endured many challenges and hardships. Once here, she worked hard, and her home and family gave her a sense of accomplishment. Being with her children and grandchildren gave her further enjoyment. Her accomplishments were simple, but they were more than what she would have had if she had stayed in Poland. She had achieved the better life she sought when she emigrated. Her life is typical of an immigrant woman, and there may be similarities to your ancestor.

Our immigrant ancestors are the foundation of our roots in the United States. Our lives would be very different if our immigrants had not endured the challenges of immigration to America. Do not underestimate their contributions. They may have left us some material wealth, but the most significant contribution they gave is their family and their role in the growth of the United States. Their lives were building blocks in the development of their new country.

Remember that they made many sacrifices for us and helped build the United States. They could not appreciate what they were doing because they worked hard and survived each day. However, what they did each day was important. Our role should be to leave something that will help our children remember them. We need to capture the memories by writing our family history.

If you are reluctant to write your family history, relax. Please write it down in your own words and voice. It should include the names, dates, and photos, and incorporate the stories and your feelings. Start with small details and then expand as you find more information. I hope my grandmother's story will serve as an example.

If you do not save
your family's memories,
Who will do it?

CHAPTER ONE - EARLY LIFE IN POLAND

My grandmother, Anna Chmielewska, is not in a history book, but her story is vital to me and should be a must-read for genealogists writing their Polish family history. She embodies the countless immigrant women who endured hardship, loss, and sacrifice before carving out a better life in America.

Anna was born at 7 p.m. on Monday, June 26, 1899, to Aleksander Chmielewski and Julia Zaluska in a small cottage in the farming village of Przezdziecko-Pierzchały, then part of Polish Russia. In Poland, fathers traditionally chose the names of their sons, while mothers selected the names of their daughters. Because of this custom, many children received the names of saints—sometimes even the saint associated with the day of their birth. However, her birthday is not near any saint's day with the name of Anna. Why my grandmother was given the name Anna remains a mystery to me.

**Picture a rural Polish home in the area
near the Chmielewski farm**

At the time of Anna's birth, families relied on an older, respected woman known as a *babka* (grandmother) or *baba* (woman) to assist with deliveries. Trained midwives were virtually unknown in rural Poland in the late 1800s, but the *babka* was trusted for her experience and skill in guiding mothers through the difficult stages of childbirth. Her role did not end with the delivery; she often continued to support the family afterward and helped introduce the newborn to the wider community.

**The Assumption of the Blessed Virgin Mary
Catholic Church in Andrzejewo**

On the day after Anna's birth, Aleksander put Julia and the baby onto his horse cart. He led them three miles down the dirt road to the Assumption of the Blessed Virgin Mary Catholic Church in Andrzejewo for Anna's baptism.[1]. Walking behind their father were Anna's four siblings – Marianna (age 17), Boleslaw (age 14), Stefania (age 12), and Hipolit (age 6). Also joining the procession were grandfather Adam Chmielewski and the godparents Franciszek and Emilia Uscinski. Emilia was Julia's first cousin, and, as godmother, she was responsible for dressing the infant for the christening. Also accompanying the family to the church were Jozef

---

[1] Baptismal record for Anna Chmielewski, Akta stanu cywilnego Parafii Rzymskokatolickiej w Andrzejewie, 1899, AKT 90

Sutkowski, age forty-two, and Aleksander Sutkowski, age forty, who were witnesses to the birth. They were farmers in Pierzchaly and brothers to Anna's grandmother, Teodora, who had died four years prior. Grandmother Franciszka Zaluska and other family members met them in Andrzejewo because they lived near the church. Babka stayed behind in the Pierzchaly to organize the christening party.

The Polish Catholic Church did not have a set time to baptize the child after birth. Healthy children were taken to the church and christened as early as the next day, but usually within a few days. However, the christening of a weak or sick child may have been put off for 3 to 4 weeks, waiting for the child to gain strength. However, a family member may have baptized a very sick child at home while waiting for the official ceremony by the priest. Anna's baptism the day after birth seems to indicate she was a healthy baby.

Father Kopalenk met the family outside the church when it arrived shortly before four o'clock in the afternoon. The priest led them into the vaulted church, where they walked down the main aisle past the rows of wooden pews. The baptismal font was at the front of the church, to the right of the main altar.

The spacious brick church was completed in 1606 and replaced a wooden structure dating from the 15th century. Behind the main altar and over the tabernacle was a large ornate canopy supported by four gold-colored columns. Under the canopy, there were three sections. A beautiful painting of the Blessed Mary is in the center above the crucifix and tabernacle. Large statues of Jesus and Blessed Mary were on pedestals in front of the other two areas. In addition, the church had two side chapels. Both are on the left side of the church under another vaulted ceiling.

**Inside the Ascension of the Holy Virgin Mary,
The Parish Church at Andrzejewo**

The baptismal font was a large marble bowl mounted on a pedestal, and there was ample space around it for everyone in the procession from Pierzchaly, as well as a few more family members from other villages closer to the church. Traditionally, the parents kept the child's name secret until the christening. Julia probably whispered the name to Anna's godmother just before departing for the church, and then to the priest there. After giving the priest the child's name, everyone was ready at the font, and Father Kopalenk baptized Anna while her godparents held her.

The customary congratulations, hugs, and kisses followed the baptism. The group then formed up outside for the return to Pierzchaly, where more friends and family, along with a celebration, awaited.

Anna's *Babka* organized the christening celebration while the rest of the family was at the church. The event welcomed baby Anna into the Polish community, and many family and friends from Pierzchaly and the neighboring villages attended.

The small farming village of Pierzchaly had seven families and about sixty villagers. Besides the Chmielewski family, their Sutkowski cousins came to the celebration along with fellow villagers, the Kruszewski, Misztalowski, Walczuk, and Wolinski families. Also attending were Anna's cousins from the Zaluska, Zaremba, Uściński, and other associated families who lived in nearby Zaluski-Lipniewo, Przezdziecko-Jachy, Lenarty, Zaręby Warcholy, Pienki Wielki, and Przezdziecko-Dworaki.

Aleksander Uscinski, age 13, a son of godfather Franciszek, attended the party. He would later play a role in finding her a husband in America. Stanislaw, age 24, another son of Franciszek, attended the party and married Anna's sister Stephania in 1907. Elzbieta Sutkowska, age 10, was also there, and she married Anna's brother, Boleslaw, in 1909.

Unfortunately, Babka's name is unknown. She was not listed in any records but was probably one of the grandmothers from the village or the larger nearby village of Jachy across the River Brok.

The *Babka* instructed her helpers to set up tables and chairs for everyone and supervised the food preparation, which included some of the family's chickens, vegetables from the family garden, marchew (carrots), kalafior (cauliflower), and *fasolka szparagowa* (string beans).

She and a handful of other *babkas* started early in the morning to fill the many pierogi needed (mushroom- and sauerkraut-filled dumplings). Shortly after her parents took baby Anna to the church for the christening, the babkas began boiling the pierogi. They used the flour that had been newly ground from grain supplied to the miller by Aleksander.

**Mother and daughter with
a ritual loaf of *Kukielki***

However, the most critical food for the christening celebration was the ritual loaf of bread (*kukielki*) that *Babka* baked. The *kukielki* loaf had soft, sweet, and aromatic dough mixed with milk, yeast, sour cream, and secret ingredients. The dough is braided into a long, decorative loaf with various patterns used by different families. The bottom crust is seared, and the top is brown, smooth, and shiny. My ancestors believed that braiding gave the bread the power to repel any evil that might surround the mother and child. In addition, folklore believed that the bigger the loaf, the taller the child would grow.

Another essential food served at the christening festivities was cheese, which my Polish ancestors also thought had the power to repel evil. There are wide varieties of Polish cheese, but the people in Anna's rural area favored the hard white *Koryciński* cheese made from cow's milk with herbs and garlic as added ingredients. It is considered the oldest variety of Polish cheese, and *Babka* had the flattened balls of cheese served as the guests began to arrive.

Additionally, guests brought more food, including Buraczki (stewed beets), sałatka jarzynowa (vegetable salad), sałatka z groszku i kukurydzy (Pea and corn salad), and *surówka z marchewki* (carrot salad). The purpose of their food gifts for the celebration was two-fold. First, it ensured plenty to eat during the festivities and afterward made food available for the weakened mother on the days after the celebration.

Besides the food, they prepared a special vodka drink called *pepkowa*. The *pępkówa wódka* has a spicy aroma and a bitter taste. It is made by mixing vodka with dried herbs, spices, and fruits.[2] It is a traditional drink for the men at the christening celebration, served with honey and sugar.

Typically, gifts for the infant were called Wiazanie (meaning "tie" or "twist") because they were tied into a corner of the diaper. Some people gave the child a copper coin if they could afford it, and the godparents usually gave a silver coin as a symbol that the child

---

[2] The mixture for *pępkówa* includes Anise fruit, cumin, angelica root, juniper fruit, calamus, coriander, allspice, bay leaf, ground ginger, cardamom, ground cinnamon, thyme, marjoram, chamomile, lemon skin,

would be wealthy and successful. Other gifts for Anna were packets of flax seeds and sewing needles, which symbolized a future housewife and the expectation that she would make clothing for her future family. Wooden crosses were also a popular christening gift.

After the servers set out the food, the singing, dancing, and music began and continued into the late evening. Nevertheless, farm work and other chores resumed the following day.

CHAPTER TWO: LIFE IN PIERZCHALY

Anna was the youngest of nine children, and her childhood quickly turned to tragedy when her father, Aleksander, died on Friday, January 12, 1900, six months after her birth. Sadly, for Anna, her father was not the only family member who died before she knew them. Additionally, four of Anna's brothers died young before her birth: Wladyslaw at birth in 1880, Josef in 1892 at age 12 months, Antoni in 1898 at age 30 months, and Jan in 1897 at age three months. Anna also never saw three of her grandparents. Her grandmother, Teodora Chmielewska, died in 1895 at age 61. Additionally, her mother's father, Franciszek Zaluska, died on September 9, 1871, at age 36, and her grandmother, Franciszka Zaluska, died in 1881 at age 47 before Anna's birth

The death of her father, Aleksander, in 1900 changed the family's structure and daily lives. As the oldest son, Aleksander would have inherited the farm. His death required grandfather Adam, at age sixty-three, to continue working full-time, including farm work and training his grandsons to take on more responsibilities. This change also signaled the beginning of a new phase in each child's life. The title to the farm would pass to the oldest grandson, Boleslaw.

Boleslaw, along with Anna's teenage sisters, Marianna and Stefania, was already helping their parents and grandfather, Adam, with the farm work. At age seven, brother Hipolit had small tasks such as weeding the vegetable garden and helping watch infant Anna. Adam may have asked his other son, Antoni, to help with the heavy work until the children matured. Antoni owned the neighboring farm and worked it with his wife and small children.

Grandfather Adam Chmielewski owned the farm where Anna and

her family lived. Their farm was small, and their home was simple and modest.

The Chmielewski home in Pierzchaly had approximately 500 square feet of space inside. The family built the exterior walls with logs from the nearby forest and filled the gaps between the layers of logs with a mixture of small sticks, rocks, and mud. The interior had wood flooring and white-painted wood paneling on the walls. The ceiling joists had wood planking installed to form a floor for the attic. The house had glass windows to let in light, but at night, candles and oil lamps were used because electricity did not reach their village until 1970. Family members carried buckets of water from the well for cooking and washing. The wood-burning stove in the center of the home served as a cooking and heating source for the entire house. The main area was large enough for cooking and eating, with a small sitting area. The room had a large table, enough chairs and benches for everyone to sit at, and a few extra chairs for guests or for sitting around the stove for warmth. Pots and pans hung from wall hooks next to shelves to store dishes. The cook used the tops of two cabinets next to the stove to prepare food and store pots and some food underneath. There were also a couple of chests to store bed linen and clothes. For drapes, a simple cloth hung over the windows. The room was very simple but comfortable.

Inside a Polish farmhouse similar to Anna's home

Initially, the house had one additional room on the main level where grandparents Adam and Teodory slept. Grandpa Adam added another room for Alexander and Julia after their marriage. The children slept in a space above the ceiling and under the thatched roof. They used a ladder to climb up to their beds at night. As an infant, Anna slept in the same room as her parents, and after her father's death, she continued to sleep with her mother. Siblings Marianna, Stefania, Boleslaw, and Hipolit shared the upper-level sleeping space.

Grandma told me, "During the winter, we all slept on the first floor to take advantage of the heat from the stove. My sisters and brothers brought their bedding down from the attic and laid their straw mattresses on the floor near the stove. Sometimes, I slept with my sisters and snuggled close to them to keep them warm. During the day, we piled the mattresses in the corner out of the way."

The second building on the property had about the same dimensions as the house and served as the barn. In addition to poles and beams, logs and chinking made up the outer walls, and thatch covered the roof. They stored the summer grain in half of the barn during the fall, winter, and spring months. During rainy and cold weather, the other half of the building housed their horse and a milk cow. Their pigs were fenced and had their own small shelters. They also had chickens that were allowed to run free and shared the barn when they chose to find shelter. They also had a root cellar near the house where they stored vegetables, fruits, jams, meats, and other foods.

They had a cow that gave the family milk, bred pigs for sale and slaughter, and about a dozen chickens for their eggs and occasional chicken in the pot for soups and stews. Their most crucial animal was their horse, which furnished the muscle to plow the fields and pull loads on the cart.

My cousin grew up in the area and told me that a typical breakfast included "zupa mleczna," a porridge-like dish made from milk and cereal grains. Their breakfast table also had fresh-baked bread, homemade butter, and honey. The honey came from the family beehives. The family drank milk from the cow and "white coffee, " a coffee substitute made from local grains such as rye or wheat.

Various soups, salads, and meat dishes were typically served for dinner. The typical soups were mushroom, peas or beans with potatoes, sour pickle with cucumbers, tomato with homemade noodles, and chicken broth with noodles. The traditional salads were *Mizeria (cucumber)*, *surówka z białej kapusty (*coleslaw), and *Surówka Warzywna (*vegetable*)*. The main dishes were *Schabowy kotlet* (pork tenderloin)*, Łowcy gulasz* (Hunter's stew), and *Kotlet mielony (minced meat)*.

The daily chores the Chmielewski children had included:
- Milked their cow twice a day
- Gathered eggs from the hens.
- Fed the horse and the chickens
- Brought water from the well to use for cooking and washing.
- Brought wood in from the pile outside for the cooking stove and heat.
- Adam, Aleksander, and the older boys fell trees to keep the wood pile supplied.
- Cleared weeds away from the vegetable crops as needed.

My grandmother Anna told me the following about her early life on the farm in Poland.

"I had to do chores when I was very little - maybe when I was 4 or 5. At first, I would put the wooden bowls and spoons out for supper, and then I helped clear the table after we ate. Very soon, I helped feed the chickens and gather the eggs in the morning.

My sister Stefania taught me how to milk the cow. After I milked, she carried the bucket of milk into the house. She married when I was eight, and I had to carry the bucket myself. After Stefania's wedding, I was the only girl left in the house besides my mother, and I became her chief helper. After that, my jobs became more important and heavier to do. I had to get food from the root cellar, stir the pots, and put wood on the stove to keep the fire hot when we were cooking.

"I had fun walking behind the plow and spreading the seed in the spring. The outside work got harder in the summer and fall. First, we pulled and cut weeds around the vegetables in the garden. Then, when the vegetables were ready, I picked them. Finally, Mama and I cleaned and prepared them for cooking or stored them in the cellar."

Grandma's family grew wheat, rye, barley, and oats for their food and to feed the animals. They used wheat for the breakfast porridge. However, the miller received some wheat and rye grains, which he ground into flour for the bread and cakes the family ate. In addition, they used the harvested barley as an essential ingredient in their daily soups and stews.

Grandma said, "The fall work was hard for my brothers and Dziadek (Dziadek is Polish for grandfather). I watched them use large blades to cut the wheat and then carry the bundles from the fields to stack them in front of the barn. They worked hard to separate the grains from the stalks by beating them on the ground. They then used large shovels to pick up the grain from the hard ground. I was not big enough to help with most of the harvest work, but they let me hold the bags as they filled them with the grains. After that, my brothers carried the bags of grain used for our soups to the root cellar for storage. I also helped my brothers bag the grain we used for our bread, but they took these bags to the młynarz (miller) to grind into flour."

I found accounts of the area describing threshing grain as the process of loosening edible grain from the inedible chaff surrounding it. Hand threshing required beating the stalks on a hard floor with a flail. Hand threshing was laborious and yielded about a bushel of wheat per hour of work.

The next step in the grain harvesting process was winnowing, separating the chaff from the grain. Farmers tossed the mixture into the air to separate the grain and chaff so that the wind blew away the lighter chaff while the heavier grains fell back down for recovery. This task required using shovels to toss the grain.

Oats were the primary feed given to livestock. They planted it in one of the strips in the spring for an autumn harvest. Another will be in the autumn for harvest in the late summer of next year. They stored the animal feed in the barn, while the root cellar held the other foods.

The straw left after separating the seeds was a by-product of the wheat harvest. In addition, the villagers used straw as a construction material to repair or add a thatch roof.

Although all family members had to work to feed the family, Anna's mother did not neglect her children's education. The 1940 U.S. Census indicated that Anna completed six years of school before being interrupted by World War I. When I was in first and second grade, Anna helped me with my reading. However, I have not found any other information about her education. Did her brothers and sisters also attend? (The 1920 U.S. Census indicated Hipolit could read and write.) Where was the school? How did she get there? How many other students?

CHAPTER THREE – MARRIAGES IN PIERZCHALY

Anna was born in the flat, quiet farmland northeast of Warsaw. Her family lived in the village of Przezdziecko-Pierzchały, set along the small, wandering river Maly Brok. An old cemetery rests on its banks, and local legend claims it stands near the site of an ancient pagan temple. In the late 1890s, Pierzchały was home to just seven families—about sixty people in all. There were no shops or merchants, only scattered farmhouses. Most farms were small, between five and ten acres, and the villagers sold their produce in the parish town of Andrzejewo, three miles to the south and roughly sixty miles (100 km) northeast of Warsaw.

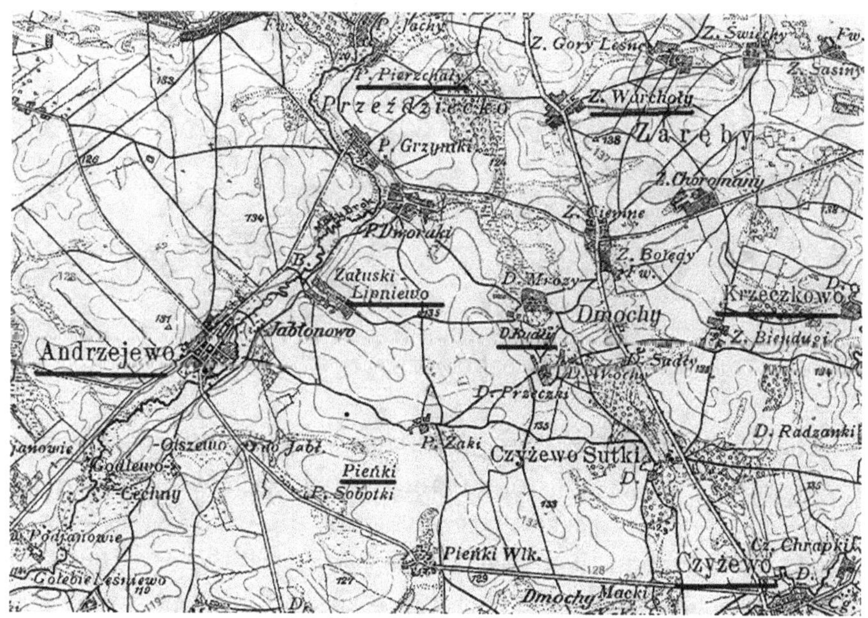

Map of villages around Andrzejewo and Przezdziecko-Pierzchaly

Today, the name Pierzchały has disappeared from modern maps. The area is now absorbed into the neighboring village of Przezdziecko-Jachy, on the opposite side of the river.

All the surrounding land once belonged to a large manor estate (falwalk) owned by the Przezdziecki family. Many villages in the region still carry a two-part name beginning with "Przezdziecko," a reminder of that estate.

Przezdziecko-Pierzchaly, 2026

Surprisingly, the birth records for Anna and her siblings show that their parents descended from nobility. However, the family did not live on a large estate or in a large manor house. Instead, they owned about 10 acres and lived a simple, modest life. The economics of owning a small farm forced her family to work the land, much like the peasants on the neighboring farms. The family worked tirelessly on their farm, and every member—Anna included, even as a small child—had chores essential to their survival.

Additionally, working their land changed the family's status. Laws governing nobility in Poland granted all nobles equal status, regardless of the size of their estates. These rules also meant that all children would benefit equally in the division of their fathers' estates. Sons inherited equal portions of the estates, and the daughters received dowries as their share. This division led to a rapid reduction in large estates, creating smaller farms that could not generate the income the nobles needed to maintain their comfortable lifestyles. The minor nobles eventually had to work in their fields or begin working for the most powerful magnates who were able to retain their economic status. However, if a nobleman contaminated himself with a plebeian occupation, such as trade, crafts, or tending their fields, the statutes governing the nobility required that he lose all his privileges as a noble.

Nevertheless, the impoverished nobles, who lost their rights, refused to accept their loss of nobility. They stood behind an invisible wall separating them from the peasants who lived nearby. They remained nobility in their minds and continued to arrange marriages for their children with partners who were also of "noble birth." They were the *zaściankowa Szlachta, or* nobles who were not recognized. They were marginalized and poverty-stricken. However, they were usually conservative, patriotic, religious, and stereotyped as provincials.

Finding *zaściankowa* Szlachta in the records for both of Anna's parents surprised me, as I had not realized they were descendants of the nobility. My grandma, Anna, told me about her life in Poland and indicated that her family worked hard on their farm. From that story, I assumed her family was peasants. However, after discovering explanations of *the szlachta, I began to understand* her life in Poland. I suspected that the traditions of zaściankowa Szlachta had a significant effect on her brothers' later efforts to find her a suitable husband.

Early Polish parents would arrange marriages for their children to protect their lands and find suitable husbands for their daughters. By the early 1900s, couples could choose their spouse, but the marriage process still included discussions with the family and always sought their approval. With the premature death of Aleksander, Julianna, and grandfather Adam, they probably became more concerned about finding a suitable marriage partner for each of the surviving children.

Once Boleslaw inherited the farm and became head of the household, there would be no room for the other Chmielewski children. So now Julia had to look seriously at what her teenage children, Marianna, Stephania, and Hipolit, needed to do to leave the family home. However, they excluded Anna from these plans due to her young age.

It was customary in Poland for the male to approach the family for his daughter's hand in marriage. He usually asked to be accompanied by the *SWAT,* who did all the talking. The initial meetings were called *wypytanie,* whose purpose was to determine if the family would welcome the man's proposal. The girl could veto continuing the discussions if she did not want to marry the man. If the family refused the man's proposal, they gave their answer indirectly so as not to insult him. If, however, the family accepted, it caused a grand celebration. The engagement was called *zaręczyny,* and the families considered it as binding as marriage. The public ceremony included tying together the hands of the bride and groom on the night of the engagement. The following day, the couple went to the priest to have the marriage banns placed. The engagement lasted three weeks while the priest read the banns during the parish church mass.

The bride married at the parish church she attended, and the celebration was festive with music and dancing that lasted at least two days.

The wedding day sometimes began with the musicians going to the groom's home to play sad tunes for him. The groom would receive his parents' blessing and then follow the musicians to the bride's home.

However, the musicians would play festive tunes at the bride's home as her friends and attendants gathered around her. The bride's friends helped by arranging her dress, hair, and veil. Sometimes, the older women joined in, chanting traditional wedding songs and admonishing the bride about her duties.

After the groom arrived, the bridal couple knelt before the bride's parents, who would sprinkle them with holy water and give them their blessing. After the blessing, the bride would receive her symbolic farewell from her parents and relatives. After the farewell speeches, the wedding party lined up for the march to the church. The musicians played for them as they left. During all this time, tears flowed freely.

The couple rode in one of the family carts to the church. As they got onto the cart, they were showered with grains of oats and sprinkled with holy water. Friends decorated the cart, and the horses and the musicians followed the wedding party in the festive procession to the church.

Anna's earliest memories of her family start in 1902, at age three, with the marriage of her oldest sister, Marianna, who, at age twenty, married Franciszek Uscinski. Next, sister Stefania, at age nineteen, married Stanislaw Uscinski in January 1907. Marianna and Stefania both found spouses from the *zaściankowa Szlachta*. Stefania's husband was the oldest son of Anna's godfather, Franciszek Uscinski, who had died in 1905.

Boleslaw found a suitable wife, and her family accepted his proposal because he was *zaściankowa Szlachta* and would inherit the family farm. At age 24, he married Elzbieta Sutkowska on July 26, 1909.

However, Hipolit had no prospects. He did not own land, and there were no jobs available for him to support a family. Immigration to America was his only option. So, in 1910, at age 17, Hipolit left for America. He worked as a butcher in Pennsylvania and New Jersey, was married, and had six children. In 1923, he returned to Poland and purchased a farm with the money he had earned in America. His family in Poland considered him rich.

Additionally, Anna's young age, fifteen in 1914, and the turmoil of World War I delayed her departure from the farm until 1921.

CHAPTER FOUR – DEATHS BEFORE THE WAR

Anna grew up not knowing her father and three of her grandparents. She remembered only her mother, Julia, and her grandfather, Adam Chmielewski, as the adults in her family.

She remembers living with grandpa Adam, her mother Julia, brothers Boleslaw and Hipolit, and sister Stephania. She remembers playing with the other small children and the party after her sister Marianna's wedding.

She told me about the funeral of her grandfather, Adam, who died in 1913 at age 76. At fourteen, she remembered her mother and other women's work preparing for his funeral and burial.

As Adam died, his family said prayers and recited litanies, asking God to help him overcome his illness. The Catholic priest came from nearby Andrzejewo to hear Adam's confession and give him the last sacraments. The family placed a scapular around his neck to protect him and placed a candle called a *gromnica* (candle flame) in his hands. This candle had been blessed at the Feast of Purification and gave hope for additional protection and peace.

Another custom that Polish families observed was ringing church bells. These bells hung outside the church and were not the main bells in the church tower. Poles called this practice *dzwonki za konajacych* (bells for the dying), and the sounds of these bells were a request to the villagers to pray for Adam and to ask God to release him from his misery mercifully.

When death came, the family observed additional customs rooted in long-held beliefs. First, the women placed Adam on a wooden plank and laid it between two chairs. Then, the body remained on the plank for three days while they cleaned and dressed it for burial. While washing the body with hot water and herbs, the women sang hymns as part of this Polish tradition.

Early death customs had the family dressing the body in a koszula śmiertelna (death shirt) gown, which was long and reached down to the ankles. Adult males had a black ribbon wrapped around their waist, neck, and wrists. In making this shirt, the tailor avoided knots in the stitching because the Poles feared the shirt would trap their sins within the knots.

When Adam died, the death shirt was no longer the custom. Instead, his family probably dressed him in his Sunday best black suit and a hat for his burial. It was also customary for Adam's body to be buried while wearing his boots.

While preparing the body, family, friends, and neighbors gathered for Adam's wake in his house. The mourners wore a black armband and prayed for his soul for three days and nights. The wake involved wailing and singing to ward off bad spirits. The singing included Catholic funeral songs and hymns.

Helpers placed Adam's body in the coffin on the day of the burial. His coffin was made from plain wood using a pine tree. The coffin had clear wood without knots and wooden pegs instead of metal nails. It was left unpainted except for a black cross in the middle of the lid. The top corners had been written, "in the name of Jesus." The bottom corners had "Heart of Mary."

The coffin was removed from the house feet first. Then, as the pallbearers moved through the doorway, they bumped the sides of the casket against the entrance three times as a means for Adam to say goodbye to his home for the final time. Finally, after his coffin had passed over the threshold, someone poured water on the ground behind the coffin. This act was a symbol to prevent the soul from returning.

Other mourners joined the pallbearers behind the coffin, which they loaded onto a cart. Then, they marched three miles to the church in

Andrzejewo for the remembrance service, asking for forgiveness for any transgression Adam may have committed.

The immediate family then proceeded with the coffin to the cemetery across the road for the burial. After the priest completed the funeral service at the gravesite, the pallbearers lowered the casket. Each mourner threw a handful of soil onto the coffin. After the burial, the family returned home to gather with relatives and friends who talked about the deceased. Then they drank vodka and ate Kasza, a barley porridge with added honey.

**Adam's burial at the Roman Catholic
Cemetery in Andrzejewo, Poland**

Unfortunately, war broke out in Europe in August 1914 and eventually affected Pierzchaly in the summer of 1915.

Between Adam's death and April 1915, Anna lived on the farm in Pierzchaly with her mother, Julia, her brother Boleslaw, his wife, Elzbieta, and his children, Josef and Janina. Her sisters, Marianna and Stefania, lived with their husbands in the nearby villages of Białe Figle and Pieńki Wielkie. Brother Hipolit had left for America and was living in Philadelphia, Pennsylvania, with his new wife.

Unfortunately, Julia died on April 19, 1915, at age 56, and the family gathered for another funeral and burial. Anna joined her brother

Boleslaw with his wife and three children, sister Marianna with her husband and two children, and sister Stephania and her husband. Julia's brother-in-law Antoni, his wife, and four children were also in the funeral procession, which went to the parish church in Ancrzejewo for the remembrance mass and then across the road to the cemetery. Julia's children now had to live without her daily advice.

Unfortunately, the war had broken out in Europe in August 1914, with the sounds of battle rumbling west of Warsaw and seventy miles (115 km) away from Pierzhaly.

Regrettably, I have not been able to find further records for the family members who remained in Poland. Polish records from this period are unavailable due to privacy laws restricting access to records until after 100 years have passed since their creation. This restriction blocks further research about Boleslaw, his sisters Marianna and Stefania, and their spouses and children. Eventually, we can add information to this portion of the family history as Poland releases sections of documents as their privacy restriction expires.

CHAPTER FIVE – THE EFFECTS OF WORLD WAR I

Anna's teenage years brought more loss and the terrifying sounds from the devastation of World War I. When asked later in life about those years, she offered only a simple, powerful answer: "We survived."

World War I dramatically impacted the Chmielewski family due to the destruction of their farm and those of others in the area where they lived. During the "War to end all wars," Poland was the main battlefield for the fighting between the Russian and German forces. At first, the major battles took place in the fields west of Warsaw. However, in August 1915, the German Army broke through and forced the Russians into a demoralizing retreat across the Polish countryside. Historical maps indicate one path of the Russian withdrawal was through the farmlands surrounding Andrzejewo.

Abandoned carts outside Andrzejewo – WWI

In August and September of 1915, the once-peaceful pastures of northeastern Poland were filled with the frightening sounds of war. The thunder of exploding artillery shells and the pops of infantry rifles replaced the usual tranquility of chirping crickets and birds. The roads became littered with the twisted wreckage of military equipment and the horrible sight of rotting, dead pack animals. The cries of panic from the Polish villagers broke through the rumble of the retreating Russian troops using scorched-earth tactics to slow the German advance. The screams meant the Russian soldiers were destroying the homes, barns, livestock, and fields of the Poles in their path. The burning of Andrzejewo and the villages in the Przezdziecko area was part of this policy, which meant disaster for the Chmielewski family when the Russians torched the homes in Pierzchaly and destroyed the Chmielewski livestock and crops.

**The destruction of Andrzejewo
during World War I**

While I was in grade school, I asked my grandmother about her life in Poland during the war. I asked, "What happened when the Russians passed through Pierzchaly? Was there any fighting near their farm? Did the Russians or German soldiers hurt anyone in the family?"

I also asked, "Were you able to find shelter? How did you find food? When were you and your family able to start rebuilding the farm?

Were you able to plant food gardens after returning to the burned-out farm?"

However, she would not tell me what happened to her or her family. Anna never answered any of my questions in detail. She would not talk about what happened. It seemed too painful. However, her only answer was, *"WE SURVIVED."*

Although Grandma did not offer an account of what happened to her family during the war, I found descriptions written by others that gave insights into life in rural Poland during and after the fighting in the Andrzejewo area.

The burning of the Polish countryside produced thousands of homeless people, and the destruction of foodstuffs and livestock created critical food shortages. The coming of winter only added to the growing hunger and suffering. When the cold weather came, frozen potatoes were the only food available.

Polish Refugees during World War I

In desperation, many hungry and homeless families fled from the burning countryside to the nearby cities, and homeless masses filled the cities. Whatever shelter the Russians had not destroyed quickly overflowed. People lie in the streets, hungry and without any belongings. City officials persuaded the reluctant German authorities to release small amounts of sugar, honey, and grain, but this did not alleviate the suffering, adequately help those sick, or feed the hungry. Eventually, officials implemented a bread rationing program, and people waited in line for hours to receive their meager portions. They also organized a free kitchen to feed the multitude of children.

Cases of typhus and cholera began occurring among the vulnerable population and grew to epidemic proportions. Only a few doctors and inadequate medical supplies were available to care for the sick. Many died. Somehow, Anna, her brother Boleslaw, his wife, Elzbieta, and their four children, Josef, Czeslawa, Janina, and Jadwiga, survived this ordeal.

After passing through the Andrzejewo area, the German offensive began to falter due to the loss of men and shortages of ammunition and food. Possibly, the Russian scorched-earth campaign was effective. By the spring of 1916, the military battles had pushed the front 270 miles eastward into traditional Russian territory. The front lines stretched from Riga, Latvia, to Ternopil, Ukraine. The fighting on the eastern front continued until the collapse of the Russian government in October 1917, caused by the Russian Revolution.

On November 3, 1918, as the war ended, the Polish people declared independence after 123 years of Russian, Austrian, and German rule. The Treaty of Versailles, signed on June 28, 1919, confirmed the New Republic of Poland. Although this act brought joy to the Polish people, the destruction from the war made life in Poland bittersweet for its people.

In January 1920, fighting broke out between a new Polish Army and Ukrainian forces, and later with Soviet forces to settle their eastern borders. The Polish Army received reinforcements from Polish-American soldiers in Haller's Army, recruited from Polish immigrant communities in America and trained in Canada. They arrived in Europe in 1917 and initially fought under the command of the French Army on the Western Front. Once the American Expeditionary Force arrived in France in 1918, the Allies transferred Haller's units to the American Expeditionary Forces under General "Black-Jack" Pershing. When the fighting on the Western Front ended, the Polish units loaded their equipment and soldiers onto trains and pushed eastward to Poland to help in the Polish-Soviet War.

The Polish forces were victorious, and as the Poles advanced eastward, the Soviets petitioned for peace and agreed to a ceasefire in October 1920. On March 18, 1921, officials signed the Peace Treaty of Riga, and the agreement divided the disputed territories between Poland and Soviet Russia

Rebuilding the Farms

Meanwhile, in 1916, rural Poland was struggling to survive. Farmers slowly returned to their farms. They had returned to plant crops needed for survival and started rebuilding their homes for shelter the following winter. Seeds were found and shared, and farm tools and implements were repaired and shared among the neighboring villagers.

Many Polish farmers found that their houses and barns had severe fire damage. In most cases, only those with stone walls were still standing. However, many uncovered small stashes of wheat and barley seeds hidden in their root cellars or buried in the nearby woods. They also found a few stray chickens who had survived, pecking at the ground around the remnants of vegetable gardens.

The returning villagers built temporary shelters using whatever walls were still standing, or the survivors moved into the root cellars while rebuilding their houses. They also devoted time to planting the seeds to have more food in the summer and fall. It was a slow, tedious process to rebuild their daily lives and survive. These efforts promised that more food would be available in the fall of 1916 and through the winter, but food shortages would persist.

In spring 1916, Boleslaw Chmielewski returned to the family farm in Pierzchaly with his wife, Elzbieta; his children, Josef, Czeslawa, and Janina; and his sister, Anna. Daughter Jadwiga and son Henryk were born in 1917 and 1920. They were the survivors and began rebuilding the farm and village with other relatives and neighbors who remained. However, repairing the destruction made their rural life more challenging than before the war.

For Anna, the changes were more dramatic. Her mother had died, and her brother's wife was now in charge of the household. Anna did not belong. It was now time for her to leave the farm.

Boleslaw had to find Anna a husband, and the lack of available single men of "noble birth" hampered his efforts. All single young men had been drafted into the Russian Army or were in the new Polish Army fighting in the Polish-Soviet War. Many did not return from the battles. As a result, Boleslaw could not find a suitable husband for Anna, and no jobs were available to support her.

Her only answer was immigration to America.

CHAPTER SIX - EMIGRATION AND VOYAGE

Anna and Boleslaw exchanged letters with their brother Hipolit to finalize plans for her to leave Poland and join him in America. Anna also began to sort her meager belongings.

She left behind one brother, two sisters, and a few cousins in Poland. All were married with children. Her parents and grandparents had all died.

Anna told my mother, "After I received Hipolit's letter telling me to come to Camden, New Jersey, I cleaned and repaired the clothing before I packed them into my suitcase. Then I looked through my other things, such as hairbrushes, pictures, and jewelry, to decide what I could take with me. The letters from Hipolit also included money I used to buy the tickets, and Boleslaw purchased a used suitcase from someone in the village.

"When the morning came to leave, Boleslaw put my bags in his cart and helped me up. He had placed a small bench in the cart for me to sit on while he walked and guided our horse the seven miles to the train station at Czyzew. We waited about an hour for the train to arrive so I could leave Boleslaw, my family, and Poland forever. I cried, and he gave me his last hug and helped me onto the train. I found a seat next to another woman, and a nice older man helped store my suitcase. I took my seat and held the bag with the food we had packed for my trip close to me. I prepared for a long journey to the harbor at Danzig (Gdańsk). The train stopped at Warsaw, and I had to get off and find the train for Danzig. The trip took all day before I got to Danzig.

"After I got off the train, an official from the shipping line loaded baggage and passengers onto a cart and took us to a room near the water where we slept that night. Then, early the next morning, we boarded our ship, which took us to England. When we got off the boat, they put us on a train to Liverpool."

**Train Route for Anna: Czyzew to Warsaw to
Gdańsk (Danzig): The trip was about 350 miles
and took 6-8 hours, which included 5 hours on the
train and the wait in Warsaw between trains.**

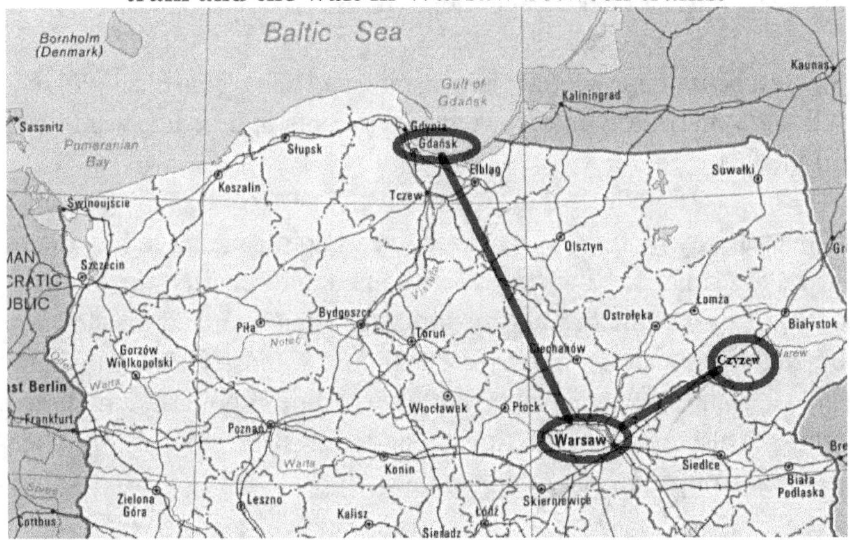

Anna had a new experience with her train ride to Warsaw. She had never been outside of the Andrzejewo area. Getting off the train in Warsaw, Anna found herself in an enormous wooden structure with a gabled roof and decorative carvings. The noise from the trains and passengers sounded strange and deafening, but she had to find the platform for the train to Danzig. Anna asked for directions, fighting back the fears from the chaos around her. Finally, she located the train, found a seat, and waited to leave. She used the time to eat some of the bread and cheese she had brought from home. The train finally left the crowded terminal with additional passengers, including emigrants like Anna, traveling to Danzig to board their ship and leave Poland and their home.

Danzig (Gdańsk) Wharf in 2012

Anna's trip from Czyzew to Danzig measured 350 miles and took over eight hours. She was tired when she arrived in Danzig and searched for the Wilson Steamship Company desk. She carefully ignored the men offering her transportation to the docks, as Boleslaw and Hipolit had warned her to avoid these thieves who would probably steal her luggage. Finally, she found the desk and showed her steamer tickets to the proper agents. They directed her and other passengers to the waiting carts, taking them and their baggage to the wharf. After arriving at the harbor, more agents led Anna and the other emigrants to dormitory-like rooms near the harbor and the ship. The room had makeshift beds set up for them to sleep overnight. They boarded their ship in the early morning after a breakfast of porridge and coffee for the next leg of their journey.

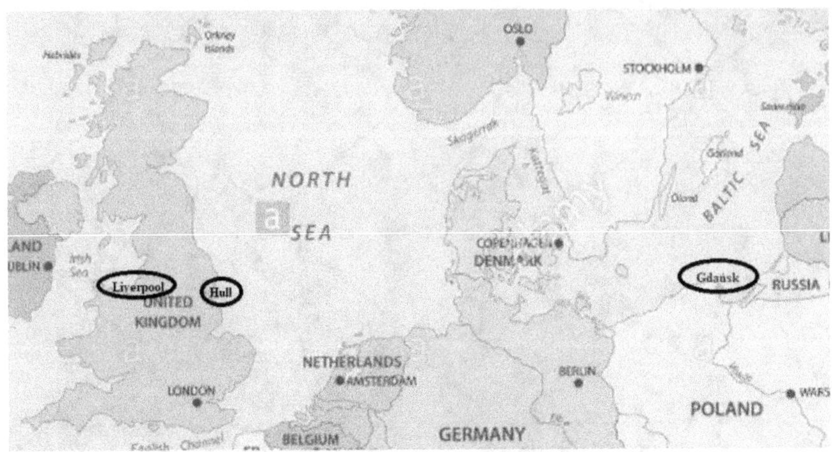

Anna left in late May when she stepped aboard a steamship of the Wilson Steamship Line of Hull, England, that took her from Danzig to the east coast of England and Victoria Pier in the Port of Hull. In the 1920s, the steamship line used four ships traveling between Danzig and Hull: SS Kovno, SS Orlando, SS Calypso, and SS Rollo.[3] All four ships were small compared to the ocean liners the immigrants would see later in their journey. You can see two ships of this class in the above picture of Victoria Pier in Hull. The SS Orlando measured 370 feet by 46 feet and 4233 tons. The Kovno displaced 1985 tons, the SS Calypso 3820 tons, and the Rollo 3658 tons. The ship Anna boarded in Liverpool was the SS Carmania, measuring 650 ft by 72 ft and weighing 19,524 tons. I believe Anna's ship was either the SS Kovno or the SS Orlando, as the other two ships were on different routes in late May 1921.

The Wilson ships hauled cargo and passengers between Norwegian, Swedish, Polish, and English ports. The voyage between Danzig and Hull covered about 1500 miles and took 3 to 4 days. She and many passengers probably had tears in their eyes as they watched their beloved homeland slip out of sight.

---

[3] https://www.theshipslist.com/ships/lines/wilson.shtml

SS Rollo (similar in size to SS Orlando and SS Calypso)

Anna's ship left Poland in the morning and made stops in Copenhagen, Denmark, and Gothenburg, Sweden, to take on passengers and cargo. The ship arrived in Hull, England, three days after departing Gdansk in the morning.

The UK Outbound Passenger List for the Carmania, departing Liverpool on June 1, 1921, indicates that Anna joined a group of 64 Poles who disembarked at Hull. The list included 9 men and 43 women traveling alone or with 12 children. The outbound list indicated the passengers prepaid for their passage on the Continent. This manifest was the only document I found explaining how Anna got from Poland to Liverpool. The maritime museum in Gdańsk told me the manifests covering Anna's departure from their port did not survive the wars and various changes of control of the port.[4]

From Hull on the east coast of England, Anna and her group took another train 150 miles across England to the port of Liverpool on the west coast of England. The group arrived after a 4-hour trip.

---

[4] Before World War I, Germany controled the port of Danzig, between the wars, it was controled jpintly by Germany and Poland, during World War II, German troops controlled the port. After the war, Poland gain sole control of the port.

Shipping line agents led them to a converted hotel where they would stay while they waited to complete medical and legal exams before they could board their ship.

Immediately upon entering the hotel, the staff disinfected everyone's body, clothes, and baggage. Next, the attendant gave her a medical inspection card with a Polish section that read, "Keep this medical inspection card. You will need to show it to American officials." She placed the card in her hidden pocket along with her other essential travel items: an exit visa, ticket, money (about $8), and the letter from Hipolit containing his address and his assurance that he would care for her in America. Anna always carefully held her coat to protect the hidden pocket and its contents. An attendant then escorted her to the women's dormitory, where she would sleep.

The women's dormitory was a vast open space, cold and dark, with row after row of triple-high cots. The smell was strange and sterile, combining the smells of travelers with luggage, boots, coats, and food mixed with antiseptic. The attendant led her to a cot and patted the gray, folded blanket, indicating this was hers. Before he left, the attendant pointed out the washroom at the end of a hall and handed her a paper with times and events in pictures - a plate of food, a red cross (for medical inspection), a bed, and another plate of food. The worker then pointed to a clock on the wall.

Anna had two hours before the first mealtime and four hours until her first of three inspections. She took full advantage of the bathing facilities before her first medical examination. A Cunard official asked her thirty-one questions and recorded them on a manifest list, the same questions Boleslaw had reviewed with her. She received two vaccinations during her second medical examination. Finally, after two days of waiting and examinations, it was time to board the ship. Beneath the covered warehouse, officials inspected the emigrants a final time before receiving a stamp of approval on their inspection cards.

Officials of the Cunard Shipping Line conducted reviews to ensure the U.S. Immigration officials approved their admission. Cunard officials feared U.S. inspectors would refuse entry and deport their passengers, resulting in a $ 100-per-person fine for Cunard and the cost of their passage back to England.

Boarding in Liverpool

On Tuesday, June 1, Anna boarded the SS Carmania and departed Liverpool, England. The SS Carmania was built in 1905 and converted into an armed merchant ship during World War I. After the war, it was refitted to carry passengers again.

Walking up the gangplank, Anna was awed by the grandeur of the ocean-going liner. A mass of people stood before and behind her. She could see the sturdy figure of the Captain with sailors scurrying to and fro amid heaps of trunks and luggage.

She produced her ticket at the top of the gangplank to give it to a sailor. He pointed to a uniformed officer, the chief third-class steward, who directed her to squeeze past the ship's machinery and descend a steep stairway to the enclosed lower decks. The immigrants milling around the third-class deck were a mixed group.

Women and girls crowded and stumbled like sheep between rows and layers of cots, nearly all in loose-fitting, dark clothing. With only a few small windows to let in the light, Anna found her berth, placed her bag on it, and covered it with the blanket. She then joined the other passengers, fleeing the stuffiness and gloom surrounding the third-class berths. Pushing past hordes of travelers, she returned to the main deck for the fresh air and just in time to hear the ship's motor chug and growl. Slowly, the SS Carmania moved away from Liverpool.

Later in the day, the ship stopped at Queensland, Ireland, where 181 more passengers boarded. Then, on June 2, they left Queensland and crossed the Atlantic, stopping at Halifax, Canada, on June 9, where one more passenger boarded.

RMS Carmania

In the early 1900s, the U.S. immigration service required all ships docking in all U.S. ports to meet strict sanitation standards that improved conditions for everyone on board incoming ships. Due to these regulations, Anna enjoyed many comforts and improved sanitation compared to the harsh conditions suffered by early steerage passengers.

Anna slept in a bed in a small cabin she shared with three other women. She and the other third-class passengers received quality food, better sanitation, and access to doctors and medication if needed. Stewards collected the pots, pans, dishes, and utensils after each meal and cleaned them by ship personnel. Restroom appliances had to be in working order, and ship stewards regularly cleaned these facilities. Stewards were also available to clean up situations caused by seasickness and other messes. The new sanitary procedures and facilities had rid the air below the ship's decks of the smell of filth, but it was still heavy and oppressive due to poor ventilation. Luckily, Anna's voyage was in June, and she could spend time on deck enjoying the fresh air.

Her passenger manifest listed her occupation as a worker. She spoke Polish and some Russian and joined many fellow Polish and Lithuanian travelers. Many passengers seemed to be Jewish shopkeepers and Jewish families emigrating from Eastern Europe. The majority of her fellow Polish travelers were workers or wives traveling to join their husbands.

Anna became friendly with some of the single Polish women in steerage. Twenty-five of them were on her trip from Gdansk to Hull. The women met on deck afternoons and in the common dining area after dinner. Many were in the same situation as Anna and left Poland because there were no jobs, husbands, or opportunities for them in their villages. They shared letters from brothers, cousins, or uncles in new lands and wondered what awaited them in America.

Polish Women Arriving
(United States Library of Congress)

Most of the women passengers had come from rural farms without indoor plumbing or electricity, and they experienced these things for the first time when they arrived in Liverpool and on board the ship. In her free time on the voyage, Anna joined the single Polish women as they shared what their letters from America had told them to expect and about their new experiences on their trip and in the harbor:

- *Many single women thought they would work as servants, but the letters also mentioned factory jobs.*

- *What was a cigar bundler? A candy packer? A mangle in a laundry? A warper, beamer, a twister, or a bobbin filler in a textile mill?*

- *Would their new homes have indoor running water like on the ship?*

- *Would the homes have the water closets they used in the immigrant compound and ships, or would they have outhouses as they had in Poland?*

- *Would the house have electricity?*

- *How would it be heated?*

Disembarking the barges at Ellis Island
(United States Library of Congress)

The married women in the third class would join their husbands, but the single women knew they had to find work in the new land and eventually find a husband. The smart ones, the strong ones, and those with strength would find a better life in America.

Anna arrived in New York on June 14, 1921. The night before arriving, she and the other third-class passengers cleaned and pressed their best clothes to wear the next day. All wanted to show their best to the immigration officials. None wanted to be rejected because of their appearance. As the third-class passengers disembarked, crewmembers hung landing tickets around their necks. Anna's tag read SS Carmania 22-19, indicating her place on the ship's official manifest, line 19 of list number 22. Finally, it came time for Anna to hug and say goodbye to her new Polish friends. Sadly, they all knew they probably would not see one another again. Finally, she disembarked with the other third-class passengers and stepped onto a barge, taking her across the harbor to Ellis Island to be processed.

The barges varied in size over the years. Those in use when Anna arrived were about 150 feet long and about fifty feet wide. The barge had two levels. After boarding the barge, Anna stowed her two bags inside the lower deck and climbed the stairs to the upper deck. There, she found a seat for the journey across the harbor. The inside of the barge had benches down each side and in the middle of the ship. Some immigrants chose to stand outside along the rail to view the Statue of Liberty and the city skyline.

Upon arriving at the Ellis Island docks, the immigrants stepped off the barges.–Uniformed men directed the immigrants across the walkways and ramps into the main building. Other officials used loud voice commands such as "Over there! This way!" and hand signals. With the passengers speaking many different languages and the immigration officers yelling and pointing many seemingly unintelligible commands at the long lines of immigrants, the tension levels within the passengers must have been sky-high. Finally, they directed the exhausted, anxious travelers into a large red-brick building. Anna followed a line of women and children under a long, covered walkway into a spacious, open area. The first phase involved getting the long lines to the baggage room, where staff somehow instructed the immigrants to leave their belongings. Next, the group followed instructions to climb the staircase to the great hall of the Registry Room.

In the great hall, Anna and the other immigrants were herded into long lines, where doctors observed them walking and checked for illnesses that needed treatment, or would exclude them from admission. As the line moved forward, doctors had only a few seconds to watch each immigrant for 60 symptoms. Then, when the medical inspectors saw possible symptoms, they used blue chalk to mark the immigrant's clothing for further examination.

The most dreaded officials on Ellis Island were the "buttonhook men" at the front of the line. These medical inspectors checked for trachoma by turning a person's eyelid inside out with a button hook to look for inflammation on the inner eyelid. This procedure seemed a harrowing experience, especially for those unfamiliar with medical examinations.

The next exam was for mental health. The inspectors at Ellis Island developed their mental tests to address the cultural differences among immigrants. This test allowed them to evaluate the immigrant's problem-solving ability, behavior, and ability to learn. The immigrants were required to copy geometric shapes, which tested if they had some schooling and were used to holding a pencil. The doctors also used comparisons and mimicry tests, which did not require an interpreter, and the immigrant did not have to know how to read or write to solve them.

Medical staff pulled passengers with chalk marks aside for a more detailed examination. Many of these immigrants passed these thorough exams and were allowed to proceed to the legal review desks to complete the entry process. However, the medical exams also determined that some immigrants had physical or mental defects, disqualifying them from entry and resulting in deportation back to the country of departure.

Medical staff took the sick with curable diseases such as measles to the Ellis Island Hospital for observation and care. Once the immigrant became healthy, they were discharged from the hospital and allowed to proceed with their legal inspection.

For the legal exams, Anna and her fellow passengers followed directions to the main part of the Registry Room, where they found a maze of metal railings dividing the entire hall. This area was overcrowded and filled with the languages of people from many countries. The inspectors stood behind their tall desks at the far end of the maze. Behind the inspectors stood an army of translators fluent in the many languages of the immigrants. The translators were there to assist the inspectors with questioning the immigrants. Each immigrant usually completed the legal exam in about five minutes, traditionally comprised of just a review of the information included on the passenger manifest the ship's officer compiled when the immigrant prepared to board. However, the entire process usually took an average of five hours for them to pass through Ellis Island.

There were over 2000 third-class passengers on Anna's ship. To her relief, officials granted her admission. She did not receive any chalk marks or need any additional examinations. However, U.S.

immigration law required a husband or male relative to meet a female immigrant. If Anna's brother were not there to meet her, they would place her in a detention area, and officials would make an effort to contact him. Detention pages for the Carmania indicate that over 200 women suffered this delay. Luckily, Hipolit learned of the SS Carmania's arrival date and met his sister at Ellis Island after she was admitted. Anna must have been tremendously relieved and excited to see Hipolit again after eleven years.

After the excitement subsided, she and Hipolit took the next step: collecting her luggage and purchasing her train ticket to Philadelphia. To start the journey to Camden, they boarded a barge that ferried them to the train station across the harbor in Jersey City. Next, they boarded a Baltimore and Ohio Railroad train that took them south through New Jersey and Pennsylvania to the main train station in Philadelphia. Finally, after changing trains, they crossed the river to Camden, New Jersey, where they transferred to a city trolley that took them south to a trolley stop a few blocks from Hipolit's house at 1231 Jackson Street.

After five weeks of travel, Anna stepped foot in America and her new home. She was tired from her trip and happy to be with her brother, Hipolit, and meet his wife and six children for the first time. On the other hand, Anna was sad to leave Poland and the family she had left behind. Then, finally, she began to remember the fear of not knowing what would happen next.

- *Would she find work? What type of work?*
- *Would she find a husband?*
- *Would she get along with her sister-in-law Stella?*

Her journey was over, but she still had many questions awaiting her. However, she felt relieved to be with her brother again after eleven years and to meet her American family members for the first time. Nevertheless, the answers were for another day.

CHAPTER SEVEN - MARRIAGE IN AMERICA

In early July 1921, the next phase of Anna's life began. This step significantly impacted the rest of her life. After arriving in America, she lived with Hipolit, his wife Stella, and his six children in Camden, New Jersey. Hipolit owned the house, which was built in 1920. It consisted of two stories, three bedrooms, and one bathroom. Anna probably shared one of the bedrooms with the three girls aged one to seven. She probably felt out of place, but family stories indicated she helped Stella with the children. A great-grandson of Hipolit told me that his grandfather, Czeslaw, had "Aunt Annie" as his babysitter.

The house was about ten blocks from Saint Joseph's Catholic Church, where the Polish residents in the surrounding neighborhood attended mass. The parish had a strong history as the social and cultural center of this Polish neighborhood.

Anna may have found work at nearby businesses or factories, but I have not seen any information to that effect. However, Anna always tried to be busy and help as much as possible. If she did work, the jobs available to single women in Camden were at a cigar factory, where women wrapped tobacco or bundled cigars. The nearby textile factory also hired women who filled the bobbins with yarn.[5]

Hipolit worked as a butcher and seemed to have a comfortable life. However, his wife wanted to return to Poland. This desire posed a family problem after his sister Anna's arrival; he now had an obligation to care for her. Hipolit and his wife's desire to return to Poland probably upset Ann and put more pressure on her to find a permanent home. The solution to this problem was to find her a husband.

---

[5] I gathered data on employers of the Polish women in Camden, New Jersey from the 1920 Federal census records.

No oral history explains how Anna and my grandfather, Steve Zuchowski, married. Still, I believe it was a combination of relationships and coincidences:

- Steve was living in Bloomington, Illinois, with Alex Uscinski, the son of Anna's godfather
- Bernice Uscinski, a daughter of Anna's godfather, married Steve's brother, Boleslaw
- Anna's sister Stephania married Stanislaw Uscinski, another son of Anna's godfather.
- Steve's cousin, Alex Dmochowski, lived four blocks from Hipolit and a few blocks from the social club at the church. They probably met at the social club and became friends, having come from the same area of Poland.

Conversations and letters among this mix of Steve and Anna's friends and relatives somehow arranged their engagement and marriage. The fit was perfect. Both were *zaściankowa Szlachta*[6] and a suitable match for one another. Although Steve did not own land, he had a steady job with the railroad. Somehow, they managed to live 900 miles apart in Bloomington, Illinois, and Camden, New Jersey. The train ride between Bloomington and Camden took 33-36 hours, so they probably did not meet before agreeing to marry. Did Steve write letters to Anna, or did he ask someone else to write his introductory letters to Anna? I believe his friend Alex Uszcienski's wife, Helen,[7] wrote his letters[8] to help with the marriage arrangements. Anna and Steve showed courage in trusting the advice and encouragement of their family members both in America and Poland.

There are many questions I wish I had asked my grandparents about how their marriage happened, but I will never get answers to these

---

[6] Descendants of Polish nobility

[7] Alex Uscienski changed his surname to Uszcienski on his naturalization papers

[8] *Records indicate that Steve had not gone to school but could read and write.*

questions. However, contemplating the possible responses gave me insight into Anna's challenges at the time of her marriage and how they affected her character.

In early July 1923, with the marriage details arranged, Hipolit took Anna to the central train station in Philadelphia. There, he said his goodbyes to her, similar to what Anna had received from her brother Boleslaw when she had left Poland two years earlier. Hipolit then helped Anna board the train at about 4:00 in the afternoon. Her trip followed the same route that her future husband, Steve, took when he arrived from Poland in 1912.

Her train, Pennsylvania Railroad #33, left Philadelphia at 4:31 PM. This train traveled west, stopping at Harrisburg and then at Penn Station in Pittsburgh, arriving at 12:16 AM. The train then continued west through the night with stops in the Ohio towns of Steubenville, Dennison, Coshocton, Newark, and Cincinnati. Sleep was probably difficult for her as the train sped through the night. Her mind was contemplating the many questions about what awaited her in Bloomington. If she did sleep, it was in her seat. If hungry, she purchased sandwiches from the "news butchers."[9] on the train. Finally, in the early morning hours, the train headed north, making a stop in Indianapolis. She was finally arriving at Union Station in Chicago at 5:00 PM the next day.

Once she arrived at Union Station, she had to switch trains. Anna walked across Union Station to find the platform for the Chicago and Alton Railroad train that would carry her southward to Bloomington, Illinois. The Number #9 train left at 6:30 PM with stops in Joliet, Dwight, and Pontiac before arriving in Bloomington at 9:45 PM. The total trip took her almost 35 hours. Since Anna had lived in the United States for two years, she could speak English and read the signs. Knowing English allowed her to make an uneventful

---

[9] Vendors who rode the passenger trains selling food, newspapers, and other sundries

but tiring trip.

Great Hall at Union Station, Chicago

Meanwhile, I believe Hipolit sold his house and returned to Poland shortly after Anna left for Bloomington, Illinois. He was not at the wedding, and the wedding was in Bloomington, not Camden. The 1923 city directory for Philadelphia listed another family living at Hipolit's house at 1231 Jackson Street.

Train Station in Bloomington

However, what were her thoughts and fears during her trip

to Bloomington?

- *She knew only Alex Uscinski in her new town.*
- *Would there be someone in Bloomington ~~that~~ she could trust to help her get ready for her wedding?*
- *Would she like the house ~~that~~ Steve rented for them?*
- *Would she find new friends to talk to during the days?*
- *Was she sure he would be a good husband? Did he drink? Would he mistreat her? (Note: I saw my grandfather drink alcohol only on special occasions, and then usually one drink, and I never saw him strike anyone.)*

Luckily, the Polish community in Bloomington was small, with about 20 families, making it a friendly, tight-knit community. Most families lived in a small two-block-by-two-block area and remained friends throughout their lives.

Alex Uszcienski (changed from Uscinski) probably met Anna at the train station and drove her to his home at 1408 West Mulberry Street. I reviewed the naturalization records for the Poles in Bloomington and found that Steve and Alex were the only immigrants from Anna's area. Although Alex probably knew both Steve and Anna before he immigrated in 1907, I believe Steve and Anna never met before Steve emigrated in 1912.

She stayed with Alex and his wife, Helen, until the wedding. The length of her trip was tiring, and it helped her overcome her anxiety and sleep that first night in Bloomington. Nevertheless, she probably nervously met her future husband the next day. In the coming days, she will meet her maid of honor and Helen's sister, Martha Zulz. Also making their way over to the Uzscienski home were the other Polish wives who helped with the wedding preparations. The influx of so many new people probably overwhelmed Anna at first.

At the Uszcienski house, Anna shared a bedroom with the three

Uszcienski daughters as Helen and her friends helped Anna prepare for the big day. Before leaving for Bloomington, she had purchased a dress in Philadelphia, but Anna's new friends in Bloomington did a final fitting and pressed it for her. The women also gave special attention to Alex's seven-year-old daughter, Bernadine Uszcienski, who was to be the flower girl.

Anna's prospective husband had been staying with the Uszcienski family since his return from the Army in 1919. However, before her arrival, he rented a house one block away on Market Street, where he and Anna would live after their marriage.

Sometime before the wedding, Steve and Anna met at the St Patrick's Church rectory with Reverend Hubert Lorinz, who later performed the ceremony. Although he knew Steve, Father Lorinz needed to meet Anna to ensure she was eligible to marry in the church and to prepare Steve and Anna for their upcoming marriage. He then read the marriage banns during the three Sunday masses before the wedding, which was his last required step in the pre-wedding process.

The diocese built St. Patrick's Catholic Church in 1892 at the request of Irish immigrants who had settled on Bloomington's west side and worked at the railroad shops. The church's first pastor was the Irish priest, Father James Burke. Although the diocese built the church for the benefit of the Irish population in the "Forty Acres," the small Polish community also attended services at St. Pat's because of its location at the northeast corner of their neighborhood.

St Patrick's Church circa 1900

On Thursday, July 12, Steve and Anna completed the last step before getting married by taking the electric streetcar downtown and obtaining their marriage license at the McLean County Courthouse.

People can easily find the church on Bloomington's west side because its spire rises well above the surrounding neighborhoods and serves as a landmark for the area. Its exterior walls are brick, and the Gothic Revival Architecture gives it a graceful feel from the 19th and early 20th centuries. Inside, it has three vaulted ceilings that rise along the sides and down the middle of the church, with the centerline being the highest. The central aisle leads to the communion rail and main altar with its gothic-style backdrop. Past the communion rail, three steps lead up to the main floor, and then there are another three steps up to the main altar. The backdrop features three spectacular Gothic spires, two statues, and a crucifix in the center. There are two more statues on each side of the central area.

Two days later, on Saturday, the wedding party gathered at the Uszcienski house on Mulberry Street. After Alex took pictures of the wedding party, they traveled the two blocks to the church for the wedding.

Steve and Anna married in St Patrick's Church in Bloomington, Illinois, on Saturday, July 14, 1923. Joseph Zulz and his wife, Martha, were the best man and matron of honor. Joe worked with Steve as a boilermaker in the Chicago & Alton Railroad shop, and Martha was Helen Uszcienski's sister.

**Steve and Anna with their wedding party
at their wedding celebration**

Upon arrival at the church, Steve and his best man entered through the side door and stood along the communion rail, waiting for Anna and her attendants to walk down the central aisle. First came little Bernadette, carrying her bouquet and slowly moving down the aisle. Next came Martha, who watched Bernadette, ensuring her niece kept walking at a good pace to the front of the church. Anna finally came bravely down the aisle as she saw many new faces in the pews who were also seeing her for the first time. After meeting at the communion rail, Anna and Steve walked past the railing and up the three steps to kneelers, where they celebrated mass, and Father Burke performed the marriage ceremony. With Saint Patrick's Church as the setting, their marriage had to be beautiful and an excellent start to their new life together.

Main Altar at St Patrick's Church

After the wedding ceremony, the reception took place a few blocks from the church, in the side yard of their new home. The Polish community in Bloomington was small, with about twenty families, and all came to the wedding celebration. Many of Steve's friends from the neighborhood and the Railroad Shops also joined the party.

The women who had helped Anna get ready for the wedding now did their best to prepare for the party afterward. Typical Polish foods, such as Kielbasa, were unavailable in local stores and had to be "imported" from Chicago. The women in the neighborhood purchased hams from local stores. They prepared traditional dishes and salads for the reception, including pierogi and Mizeria (cucumber), surówka z białej kapusty (coleslaw), and Surówka Warzywna (vegetable). Steve hired a band that knew how to play some polka songs.

Sharing bread, salt, and wine is an old Polish tradition. At the wedding reception in Poland, the bride and groom's parents would greet the newly married couple with a goblet of wine and bread lightly sprinkled with salt. Hopefully, a more senior Polish couple, such as John Kopka and his wife (Helen and Martha's parents), performed this tradition.

The bread represented a hope that the couple would never be hungry. The salt reminded the couple that they might experience difficult times and that they must learn to cope with life's struggles. The wine was to wish the couple a happy life, good health, and never to be thirsty.

WEDDINGS

Zuchowski-Chimielewski

At eight o'clock Saturday morning, in St. Patrick's church, took place the marriage of Miss Anna Chimielewski, of Camden, N. J., and Mr. Steve J. Zuchowski, of Bloomington. Rev. Hubert Lorenz, of Peoria, read the ring ceremony. Miss Gadd played the wedding march, and sang three solos appropriate for the occasion. The attendants were Mr. and Mrs. Joe Zulz, while the flower girl was little Bernadine Uscienski. After the ceremony a wedding breakfast was served at 1316 West Market street, which is the new home of Mr. and Mrs. Steve J. Zuchowski.

**The Pantagraph, Bloomington, Illinois,
July 16, 1923, Monday, Page 8**

Steve and Anna began dancing, and then Anna had to dance with every male guest. Finally, the dancing was interrupted for supper, then resumed for the evening. The traditional capping ceremony was probably held late in the evening after supper and much dancing. For the ceremony, Anna sat in the middle of the room, with the guests standing in a large circle. One of the matrons took off Anna's veil.

Friends usually took up a collection for the bride and groom instead of gifts. They used the collection to help pay for the wedding and to leave a comfortable nest egg for Steve and Anna. For example, I believe they received silver dollars from this collection. After Grandpa's death, Grandma gave me about a dozen silver dollars dated 1923. I am sure these coins were part of the collection from their wedding.

Did Anna and Steve's reception last for more than a day? This was a Polish custom and was true for other ethnic groups living in Steve's neighborhood. However, I do not have reliable information to confirm it did or did not." Additionally, some of their traditions were missing from this celebration. Nevertheless, pictures showing the wedding party at the reception indicate a bright, sunny day, so everyone indeed enjoyed the outdoor party.

After the celebration, Steve and Anna settled into their rented home at 1316 W Market Street to begin their new life.

CHAPTER EIGHT - NEW LIFE IN AMERICA

After their wedding celebration, Steve and Anna began their new life in a rented house at 1316 W Market Street. The house was small, at about 850 square feet, with two bedrooms and one bathroom. It had a small side yard and was near the neighborhood grocery store. Their first child, Regina, was born there in May 1924.

In 1926, they purchased the house at 1418 West Mulberry. Their second child, John, was born there in 1927. This home was the same size as the Market Street structure and also had two bedrooms and one bathroom. The added benefit of owning this home was the gardens. Family photos show that Anna had at least three areas where she planted roses, a passion she developed. Steve and Anna lived in this house for over 20 years.

In addition, I found a death certificate for a third child who was stillborn in 1935. The record indicated that the unnamed boy was buried at St. Mary's Cemetery in Bloomington. I never knew about this baby boy, and it surprised my sister when I told her. Apparently, it was too painful for my grandmother to talk about her little, lost boy. The death of her baby was another tragedy she endured.

A notice in the local newspaper, the Pantagraph, indicated Anna would be a hostess at a club meeting in May 1938 for the Day Nursery and Social Settlement Association. The Day Nursery, located at 1320 W Mulberry, was one block east of where Anna lived. Although I have not found evidence that Anna worked during the 1930s, she may have worked at a nearby business and needed the Day Nursery for her 11-year-old son, John, before and after school. She would only have been able to work part-time, as she still had responsibilities as a mother to John before he left for school and when he returned. Nevertheless, the 1937 and 1938 city directories did not list an occupation or employer for Anna.

**Day Nursery
Mothers to Meet**

The Day Nursery Mothers club will meet at 2:30 p. m. Friday at the Day Nursery. Mrs. Eugene Crawford and Mrs. Anna L. Zuchowski will be hostess.

From the Pantagraph, May 26, 1938

Husband Steve had steady work at the railroad shops even during the depression years, when many people were unemployed, and families struggled. As a boilermaker's helper at the Chicago & Alton Railroad repair shops in Bloomington, his work did not require great skill, just hard work and muscle. Still, his labors were essential to maintaining the railroad's steam locomotives. He worked on the boiler of a railroad steam engine, which required more maintenance than any other part of the locomotive and was the most expensive to maintain.

He worked there until he retired in 1949, with his only loss of work occurring during the three-month rail workers' strike in 1923. During the depression, Steve saw steady employment, and the shops did not significantly reduce his hours. In the early 1930s, he earned about $ 1,200 per year, which increased to $ 1,800 in 1940 and $ 3,200 in 1948.

Another significant event for Steve and Anna was the purchase of a new car that my grandfather drove with great pride. Family pictures show the car was a 1941 Packard, model 120 four-door sedan, considered a luxury automobile. In addition, the Packard Car Company was considered a leader in technological advances and body design.

**Packard 110 Sedan Series 1700
Luxury Model- 6 cylinders, four doors**

A new advancement that may have been on grandpa's car was the Econo-Drive transmission introduced in 1939, a kind of overdrive. Another was the Handishift, which put the gear shifter on the steering column. With great pride, Grandpa made the Packard the background of many family pictures from 1941 to 1949. The photos included family outings at local lakes and trips to Chicago to see friends and relatives.

Family pictures indicate that Anna returned to Poland to visit her family in 1938.

**Anna and her nephew
Stanley Chmielewski were
born in 1938 in Czartosy,
Poland**

I found a photo of her with her nephew, Stanley Chmielewski, that appears to have been taken in Poland on March 29, 1938. The inscription on the back of the picture was in Polish and translated as "*My sweetest aunt, in memory of a very cold afternoon, Stach Chmielewski – Czartosy June 29, 1938.*" Czartosy is located in Lomza Powiat (province), about 6 miles north of Andrzejewo and just south of Zambrow.

The picture was probably taken in the church courtyard in Zambrow, about 6 miles north of Andrzejewo. Anna probably visited with her brothers, Hipolit and Boleslaw, and her sisters, Marianna and Stephania, during this trip, but I have not found any pictures to confirm this.

Stanley had been born in Philadelphia before his parents returned to Poland in 1923. He returned to the United States in 1939. His parents and his siblings stayed in Poland and somehow survived the turmoil of World War II.

Here are some important events that happened in Anna's life in the 1940s:

- In March 1943, her daughter Regina married Marty Szabados while he was serving in the Army Air Corps.
- Anna became a naturalized citizen in McLean County Circuit Court on May 22, 1943.
- Son John waited until he turned 18 in 1945 to enlist in the Navy and served on a supply aircraft carrier off Japan at the war's end.[10]

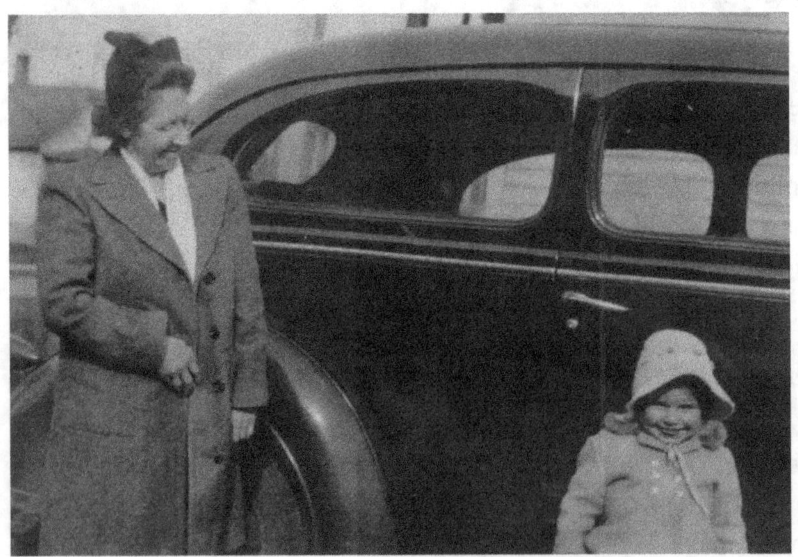

Anna with granddaughter Geneen about 1946,

---

[10] From John's Naval service records

Grandpa's luxury Packard car is in the background.

- After the war, Anna began sending packages of food and clothing to Poland. I do not know if this was to relatives or one of the Polish relief organizations. I was very young at the time, but I thought I heard my grandmother talking as if the packages were going to family members.

Europe suffered significant destruction during World War II, and Poland was one of the worst affected. The devastation caused widespread hunger, homelessness, and suffering. Recovery in Poland was even slower because of the reluctance of the Polish Communist officials to accept aid from the West. Polish Americans gave food and clothing to their local Polish groups, such as the Polish Relief Committee in Wisconsin, the Polish Roman Catholic Union in Chicago, and the Polish Women's Alliance. Most of the material went to groups in Europe outside Poland, such as the Paderewski Hospital in Paris, with the hope of delivering to groups in Poland.

The Hospital Notes in the Bloomington Pantagraph indicate that Anna was ill in the years following the war. Notices in the paper stated Anna was in St. Joseph Hospital on October 8, 1945, January 19, 1946, and July 30, 1947. In addition, I remember stories from my mother telling me that my grandmother was very sick because of her gall bladder.

Unfortunately, Grandpa Steve suffered a stroke in March 1949 and was off work for eight months. He tried returning to work in November, but they granted him a disability pension, and he officially retired.[11] I remember my mother telling a family member that Grandpa had three strokes.

---

[11] From Steve's Railroad Pension papers

With both Steve and Anna having health problems, Regina wanted to be near her parents to care for them. To help with this goal, Steve and Anna purchased a larger home and a few houses up the street from their home. The plan was for daughter Regina, her husband Marty, and their two children to live with Anna, Steve, and their son John.

On November 3, they purchased the home at 1409 W Mulberry for $2800. This house was an upgrade in size from the house at 1418 W Mulberry. The house was also across the street from their friends Alex and Helen Uszcienski.

The new house had more bedrooms and space, especially in the kitchen, where a large table would allow the family to eat. The main benefit of the purchase was the extra bedrooms to accommodate the whole family. Still, Anna was also excited about the spacious backyard and side lot, which would expand Anna's gardening efforts.

The House at 1409 W Mulberry Street, about 1953

The house was two stories and was built in 1831. It had seven rooms, one bath, and a basement. The one bathroom and kitchen were part of an addition that previous owners added to the back of the house. The kitchen was large, with cabinets, a sink, a stove, and a refrigerator along one wall. We used the space opposite the cabinets for the dining table, which easily seated all seven family members. One side wall had a window where Grandma's Singer sewing machine stood. There, she repaired shirts and pants and sewed her quilt squares together. Her African violets in small pots sat along the kitchen windows. The number of African violets increased over the years, even though she gave some away as gifts.

**Grandma's Kitchen
at 1409 W Mulberry – 1950s**

**Grandma had a Singer Pedal
Sewing Machine in the Kitchen**

The original first floor included two bedrooms, a living room, and a second large room. We initially used this as a formal dining room and later as a family area where Steve could watch TV. The second floor had two large rooms. We used one of the two rooms on the second floor as a bedroom. Regina, Marty, and the grandchildren slept in the upstairs bedroom. We used the second room on the top floor as the TV room after Marty purchased a TV in the early 1950s.

The TV provided the family with many enjoyable nights watching the Lawrence Welk Show on Sunday evenings and the Saturday Night Fights. In addition, I enjoyed the sounds and images from cartoons and western TV series such as Hopalong Cassidy and the Lone Ranger on Saturday mornings.

Anna used the main room in the basement to do laundry. She used a wringer washing machine and hung the clothes to dry in the large room under the living room during the winter months. She used the gas stove and the work counter to harvest the summer vegetable crop. The space under the bedrooms housed the furnace, which Marty had converted from coal-burning to oil.

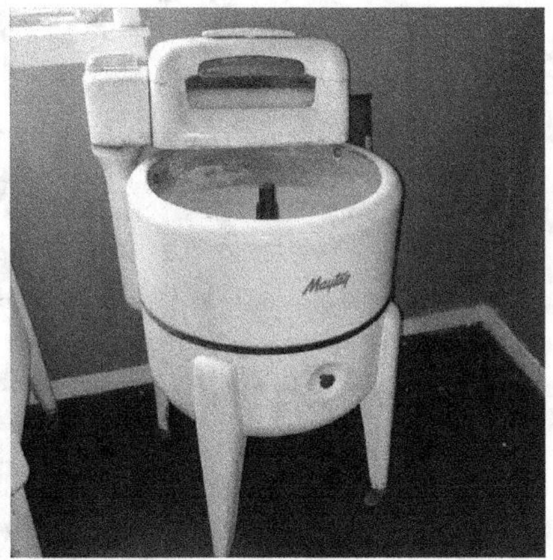

1950s Wringer Washer Anna and daughter Regina used in the Basement for laundry

Anna's Rose Garden at 1409 W Mulberry

I believe that the backyard was Anna's favorite place because of her rose garden. Her roses covered most of the garden area with over fifty different rose bushes, and this was where she devoted most of her time during the summer. In the late 1950s, I was my grandmother's main helper in her garden. She had me dig the hole when she added a new rosebush. Anna supervised the digging to ensure each hole was dug to the correct depth and width. When it was ready, she carefully added some of her enriched soil and then asked for her teapot (*czajniczek*), which she used to pour water into the hole. Dirt was backfilled and gently tamped down, and she then added more water around the newly planted rose.

The garden also had many food sources essential to the family table. There were raspberry bushes along the back fence, and in front of them was a huge patch of strawberries. Between the strawberries and the rose bushes, Anna planted tomatoes, onions, cabbage, carrots, corn, green beans, and other vegetables she used in the family meals. Tomatoes were a significant product in her canning jars. Water for the garden came from rainwater collected in a large underground cistern, and we used a hand pump to fill buckets to water the plants. The purchase of the house included a second lot that, for a few years, was used to plant sweet corn.

There was a grapevine on a trellis along the west side of the garage. The home's previous owners were German immigrants from the Moselle wine area. I now see they probably cultivated the grapes, hoping to make wine. Unfortunately, my family never utilized the grapes very well. We did not like their taste, and my grandparents did not try to make wine.

I also remember an apple tree next to the drive and garage. Grandma used the apples to make the many apple pies she baked, which were a special treat served at dinner.

They had a two-car garage, and behind it stood a wooden shed. In the 1950s, my grandparents kept chickens in the fenced area between the shed and the garage. We picked eggs from the nests inside the shed, and occasionally, I watched Grandma pluck the feathers from a chicken headed for the family dinner table. Fried chicken and chicken soup were frequent items on the family menu. Anna always saved the neck for herself. Then, in the late 1950s, the city ordinance was changed to bar chicken coops within the city limits. So we stopped raising chickens, demolished the shed, and removed the fencing.

There was a small cherry tree along the west side of the house. I think my grandparents planted it after they purchased the home. I remember it yielded a small crop of cherries that the neighborhood birds and I enjoyed. But unfortunately, very few cherries made it inside the family table because I ate so many from the tree.

Anna dressed for church.

Steve and Anna, about 1950, in front of 1409 W Mulberry

The 1950 census indicated that Anna and Steve lived at 1409 W Mulberry with their son John, daughter Regina, and her husband Martin, and grandchildren Geneen and Steve. Grandpa Steve worked at a restaurant washing dishes. His son John, daughter Regina, and son-in-law Martin worked at St Joseph's Hospital.

Paperwork in Steve's military file included a December 1950 request from the VA regarding a medical emergency. This document was probably to verify the benefits so Steve could stay at a VA hospital while he recovered from one of his strokes. I remember visiting him in a medical ward at a Veterans Hospital about this time. I was 3 or 4 years old at the time. My mom told me Grandpa was very sick, but I was too young to know what was happening.

Steve and Anna with grandchildren about 1955

Anna spent most of her life at home, keeping house for her husband and children. However, she did work outside the home a few times. The 1941 city directory indicated that Anna worked as a maid for the Illinois Hotel. In the early 1950s, I remember seeing her work in the laundry room at St Joseph's Hospital, and in the late 1950s, she worked in the kitchen of a neighborhood restaurant (Auth's Restaurant at 1401 W Market). I remembered enjoying the catfish dinners she brought home.

**Auth's Restaurant
Circa 1950**

Auth's ad circa 1960

**Anna is in her garden at
1418 Mulberry.**

**Anna's friend Cecilia
Claussen**

Her friends included Edna Schultz, who was Polish and lived three houses down the street at 1413 W Mulberry. Edna's husband worked with Steve at the C & A shops. Another friend was Cecilia Claussen, whom Anna met while working at St Joe's Hospital and lived down the block at 1423 W Mulberry. She also stayed close to Helen Uszcienski, who lived across the street. Another friend was Bertha Meyer, who had moved to Lakeland, Florida, after her husband, Ray, retired. Family pictures indicate that Anna made at least one trip to Florida about 1940, and photographs suggest that Bertha and Ray returned to Bloomington to visit at least once.

Steve and Anna lived on Mulberry Street until Steve died in 1964. After his death, Anna moved to her daughter's new house on Bloomington's east side. This move was logical because of her husband's death and her deteriorating health. She had short hospital stays in 1961 and 1963. The move also meant someone would be around to help care for her day and night.

However, it was also a tough decision because she would be away from her beloved garden. To offset her sadness, we transplanted many of her rose bushes to the backyard of my parents' house. However, this effort failed as her health quickly deteriorated, and she lacked the strength to tend her flowers.

Sadly, Anna died in her sleep on January 4, 1965, at age 65, less than eight months after Steve's death. The cause of her death was heart failure. The funeral mass was at St Patrick's Church, and her burial was at St Mary's Cemetery next to her husband's.

Thoughts to remember Anna

Anna was physically small, standing 4 feet 10 inches and weighing about 90 pounds. Still, she had the strength to survive the tragedies of her early life in Poland and the fortitude to overcome the challenges of starting a new life in America among strangers and to build her family. While Anna was alive, she worked hard and was the primary caregiver as her husband's health deteriorated.

While I was growing up, the meals at the Zuchowski table were hearty and simple but lacking in Polish tradition. Grandma always served basic meat, vegetables, and potatoes. When I later learned about Polish foods, I thought Anna's non-Polish menu was due to Bloomington's lack of Polish groceries. However, I now believe that the events of World War I may have prevented Anna from learning Polish cooking from her mother. As a teenager, she was learning to survive during World War I. Her mother died when she was sixteen, Russians destroyed her home, and starvation and sickness surrounded her family during the winter of 1915. Fortunately, she survived.

Her life had been harsh in Poland, but in America, she overcame more challenges and somehow found happiness. The main hobby in her new home was tending her African violets in the kitchen windows and the backyard rose garden. She also made quilts using her treadle-powered Singer sewing machine. On Sundays, Anna walked two blocks to attend mass at St Patrick's Church. She also visited with her Polish neighbors when she could. Another enjoyment was playing gin rummy with her grandson, Steve.

These were simple activities that gave her peace, enjoyment, and happiness. She had earned these pleasures together with many years of hard work.

My memories of my Grandma Zuchowski:

- *Our mother worked, so Grandma Zuchowski (Anna) watched my sister and me during the day. I do not remember what I did with her during my early stay-at-home years, but I know I kept Grandma busy. There is one picture of me and her standing in the doorway. And I had one foot outside, and she was trying to put on my pants. I must have been determined and in a hurry to go out to play.*

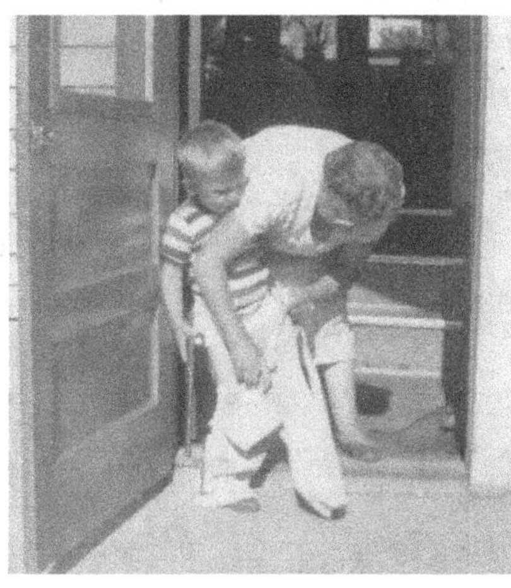 

- *After I started school, Grandma taught me how to play Gin Rummy. We played after the housework was done and before she began dinner. I remember many quiet afternoons playing this card game with her. I think she let me win sometimes.*

- *Another afternoon activity with her was planting another of her many rose bushes. Again, her garden dominated the backyard, and her roses occupied over half the space. My job was to dig the hole for the rose bush that grandma pointed out, fill her teapot (czajniczek) with water from the handpump, and refill the hole around the new rose bush.*

- *My grandparents raised chickens for eggs and meals. There was a chicken coup and a fenced-in area behind the garage. Grandma let me go in the pen, feed the chickens, and help collect the eggs. Once I followed her into the pen, I watched her grab one of the chickens and twist its head. She then put it in a bucket of water to soak before plucking the feathers. Grandma told me this would happen, and I knew the chicken would be dinner the next day. Shortly after, the chickens disappeared because the city changed its ordinance and no longer allowed livestock within the city limits.*

- *After starting at St Pat's School, I began walking with my grandmother the two blocks to St Patrick's Church for Sunday Mass. This walk was always pleasant in good weather, and I would ramble on with stories about various topics that she would patiently listen to and sometimes comment on. She was always very patient with me.*

- *I remember going to the grocery stores with my mom and grandmother. My mother and grandmother did most of the shopping at supermarkets, where I would ride in the cart as they would fill it with food.*

- *We also shopped at Devary's, a neighborhood store, for fresh meat and daily needs. When I got older, Grandma sent me to Devary's for bread and milk. I remember how proud I was to ask the saleslady and then hand her the money to pay for it. She had to remind me to wait for the change.*

- *In the late 1950s, Grandma worked in the kitchen at Auth's, a local restaurant. She brought home a catfish dinner, a leftover from their weekly fish fry one night. The dinner was the first time I had catfish, and I liked it. After that, I would occasionally stop at Auth's kitchen door when she was working, hoping to get another taste of catfish.*

- *I also remember my grandmother sewing at her Singer sewing machine, piecing together the squares for a quilt. Grandma drove the sewing machine by moving a foot treadle, and I was amazed by how quickly she put everything together.*

- *My mom and grandmother washed clothes in the basement using an old-style wringer-washer. Then, they hung the clothes on lines outside the backyard to dry in warm weather or on lines in the basement when the weather was cold or raining.*

- *The basement laundry area was also the canning area, where the tomatoes and other produce from the garden were cooked and preserved for winter use.*

- *Dinners at the Zuchowski table were very basic. Grandma did not bring any Polish recipes from the old country with her. Our meals consisted of meat, potatoes, and vegetables. However, I was picky about what foods I liked to eat. My favorites were ham, hot dogs, hamburgers, chicken legs, mashed potatoes, cream corn, and pork and beans. When these foods were not on the table, Grandma would make something special for me. Later, I was frustrated when my children were picky, but I understood my grandmother for spoiling me.*

Christmas at Grandma's

My Polish grandparents told us about their festive Christmas celebrations in Poland, which included Christmas Eve dinner, caroling, storytelling, and midnight mass. However, Christmas Eve in Bloomington, Illinois, was far less festive. Dinner was light and easy to prepare, allowing the adults to finish wrapping presents and preparing for Christmas morning's magic. Everyone also had to rest, then get ready to attend midnight Mass at St Patrick's Church. I tried to be good and stay awake during mass. The Christmas songs always helped. Once home, it was easy to fall asleep and wake up the following day, excited to see what was under the tree. I enjoyed opening my presents and even got a Red Rider BB gun one year. However, I never got the Lionel train set that was always on my Christmas wish list. Grandma sat back and watched as we all opened presents, and she was always pleased and excited about what she received. One year, she was extra excited when she opened her gift and found a silverware set in a velvet-lined wooden storage case.

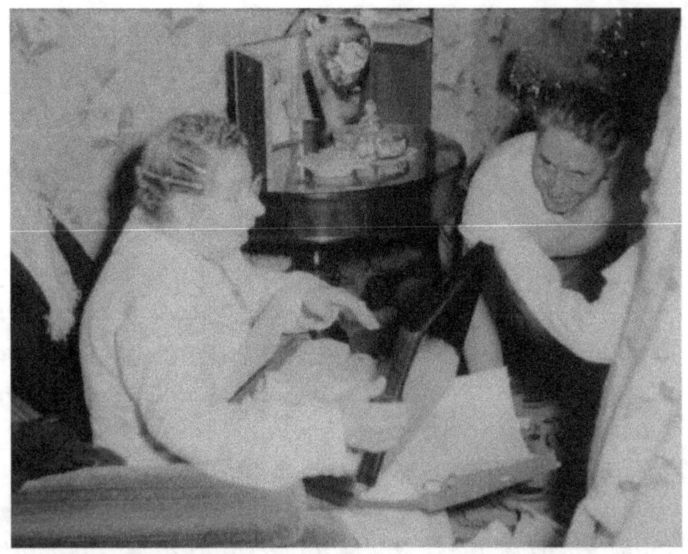

Anna is getting a silverware set at Christmas.

We opened the presents, picked up the wrapping, and put it away, and it was time to celebrate at the Christmas table. Ham was the main course, cooking in the oven while we opened the presents. Next, Grandma put mashed potatoes and a vegetable on the table. I do not remember much about the vegetables because I concentrated on ham, mashed potatoes, and dessert, usually apple pie and ice cream.

Our Christmas was not a Polish Christmas, but it was my Christmas memories with my Polish grandparents.

Save the Memories of your Ancestors

Anna will not appear in any history books. Still, her story is remarkable because she was one of the many Polish women who immigrated to the United States and enjoyed a family and a better life. Her story is an example and, hopefully, will be used by the many descendants of other Polish immigrants to understand their grandmothers' immigration and to expand their family histories beyond a collection of names and dates.

Think about your ancestors and the memories you want to pass along to your children and grandchildren. Please write them down and save them so they will not be lost.

We all have family stories that give insights into the lives of our ancestors. Some are entertaining, and others are historical. Many others are celebrations of our ethnic and cultural heritage. Unfortunately, pieces of these stories are lost as families pass them down from generation to generation. Writing a family history will save it for many generations.

You may hesitate to write down these stories because you do not consider yourself a writer or see how your family history is essential to saving. However, you need to understand that someone in your family should capture and preserve the oral histories, conduct research to confirm the accuracy of the story, and conduct research to increase the knowledge of your ancestors' lives. Our immigrant ancestors contributed to America's history; we should save their stories for our grandchildren. Our family histories should provide clues about our roles, helping us understand our roots.

APPENDIX: HOLIDAYS AND CUSTOMS

Celebrating holidays and special events gave the Polish people an overall rhythm to their lives during the year. My Chmielewski family enjoyed this rhythm as the seasons and weather changed. Their extended family and neighboring villagers would come together to celebrate customs for different holidays in each season. The festivities relieved them from their daily work and gave them a festive time to look forward to. The following are descriptions of some important holidays celebrated in Przezdziecko by the Chmielewski family and their village. Remember that many holidays were related to the beginning or end of the seasons.

Winter – Christmas

We all love Christmas because of its magical atmosphere. It is a particular time when people forget all their problems and try to be together. Christmas helps people transform themselves from the cold, dark realities of winter into a better state of mind by enjoying the festive celebrations. As a result, family, relatives, friends, neighbors, and strangers become kind, friendly, and generous.

Thoughts of the Christmas festivities began with the four weeks of Advent, which serve as preparation for Christmas through fasting and prayer. Then, at the start of the holiday season, the homemakers in the Przezdziecko area began cleaning their homes and preparing those special dishes and treats such as Christmas cakes.

The Christmas trees are set up in most homes on Christmas Eve, but not in all. Houses like the Chmielewski family in Przezdziecko were families where their four children especially enjoyed the Christmas tree. The trees were hung from the ceiling and decorated with walnuts wrapped in silver and gold foil, bright red apples, gingerbread in fancy shapes, and chains made of glossy colored paper. In addition, a manager was appointed at the church in Andrzejewo and at the Chmielewski home. The children made many decorations each year, but Anna's parents used the manger and some foil decorations for many years.

For Christmas Eve supper, they placed straw or hay under the tablecloth and used it after the meal to tell fortunes. In addition, sheaves of each of the four principal grains were placed in the room's corners in this farming area. Another interesting custom was setting the table for an odd number of people, no matter how many attended.

They watched for the first star to appear because it was the signal to begin supper. After sighting the star, those attending the Chmielewski celebration knelt in prayer. Next, the breaking of the Christmas wafer (*opłatek)* started by passing it to each person at the table. After each person broke off a piece of the *opłatek*, they exchanged holiday wishes in the form of prayers, such as "God bless you" or "God give you happiness" - "Daj Ci Boze szczescie." The *opłatek* were unleavened wafers made from pure wheat flour and water, usually rectangular and very thin. They were identical in composition to the communion wafers used in the Catholic Mass. The *opłatek* at the Christmas meal was a reminder in the home of the Polish villagers. The Opłatki wafers were embossed with Christmas-related religious images, varying from the nativity scene, especially the Virgin Mary with baby Jesus, to the Star of Bethlehem. After they passed the wafer around the table, everyone tasted the traditional dishes. Each dish followed the rule to use food from the family's food sources – grains from the field, vegetables from the garden, fruit from the orchard, mushrooms, and herbs from the woods, and fish from the sea, river, and pond. The meal included cheese, sauerkraut *pierogi*, fish in various forms, fish or mushroom soup with noodles, herring, boiled potatoes, dumplings with plums and poppy seeds, stewed prunes with lemon peel, a compote of dried fruit, and poppy seed cake appear.

After supper, the candles on the tree were lit by the entire family or sometimes by only the children. Then, the whole family joined in singing Christmas carols. After that, the grandfather, Adam, or mother, Julianna, would tell old Polish Christmas legends and different stories of how Christmas was celebrated in ancient times. One favorite story was the belief that the farm animals spoke in human voices at midnight.

Beginning on Christmas Eve and continuing through the holidays, groups of boys from Przezdziecko and the two nearby villages went around singing Christmas carols for their neighbors. They usually carried a *szopka,* a miniature stable, with figures of the Holy Family, the shepherds, and the animals mounted on a pole or a platform and carried shoulder-high. One person in the group carried the star and was the *gwiazdor, star boy,* or star man. Over time, the person who carried the star became known as jolly St. Nick.

The evening's festivities ended with the family blowing out the candles and traveling to Czyzew to attend midnight mass.

On Christmas Day, the Chmielewski family spent the day at home eating, singing, and enjoying the family. Then, they visited friends and family in the neighboring villages on the second day of Christmas.

New Years
Like many holidays, the New Year's celebration begins the evening before. In rural Poland, fortune-telling was a favorite activity this evening. Many methods were practiced, but all sought to foretell future marriages, deaths, good crops, and christenings. Another custom the young boys practiced was marching around the fruit trees. They were trying to awaken the trees from their winter sleep by clanging pots and pans or ringing bells.

On New Year's Day, Polish people usually visit their friends and relatives to offer their best wishes on this important day. The typical greeting was "bóg cię stykaj," which translates to "God's good graces touch you."

New Year's Day and the Twelfth Day of Christmas were essential days in the winter cycle, and as with many Polish holidays, the Poles baked special bread for the occasion. The ritual bread for New Year's celebration was called *nowe laki* and baked on the evening before New Year's from rye or wheat, but wheat was preferred because it gave a smoother consistency. The bakers worked the dough for the *nowe laki* bread loaf longer than regular bread to make it denser. This practice made the bread harder after baking, allowing the baker to make the dough into small, detailed shapes. For example, before baking, they tore off small clumps of dough and formed into figures of farm animals, fish, fruit trees, men on horses, hunters with the game, and women with children. The hardness of the bread also allowed the figures to include many details.

After baking, the villagers hung the figures from the rafters or above the stove or fireplace. They were left hanging there throughout the year unless needed for a sick or breeding animal. To prepare the dough figures for use, the Poles soaked them in water before baking.

The Feast of the Three Kings or the Feast of the Epiphany
The Polish people celebrated the Feast of the Three Kings twelve days after Christmas. They began the day before by baking a special wheat bread called szczodraki, offering to visit friends and give to needy children who came caroling. They also distributed it to the poor. The baker shaped the bread into various figures, including farm animals, people, and stars.

During the evening before the Feast of the Three Kings, the Chmielewski family usually sat around the fireplace singing carols and waited for the carolers to stop outside their modest homes. Instead, the carolers would come to the door to offer best wishes for a bountiful year and to sing memorable songs. The family may have seen two groups of carolers. One was the village's poor children, and the second group was the *Gwiazdory,* who came dressed in unique costumes to represent the three Wise Men.

The following day, the family hurried to church carrying a small box that contained resin, juniper berries, a piece of chalk, and gold foil. The priest blessed the box and then took it home. After returning home, the *gospodarz* (Adam – the head of the house) used the chalk to write the letters KMB, separated by crosses on all the home doors. The letters represented the initials of the Three Wise Men – Kasper, Melchior, and Baltazar. This practice was to protect the family from illness. In addition, rubbing the necks of the family with the gold foil was thought to prevent sore throats, and the juniper berries were burned as incense in the house and stables to add protection for the animals and family.

The Feast of the Three Kings ended the twelve days of Christmas and signaled the beginning of *zapusty* or carnival time, which lasted up to Ash Wednesday.

Spring – Lent, Palm Sunday, and Easter
Ash Wednesday signaled the end of *zapusty* and the beginning of the forty days of Lent. This time was a solemn period of fasting and prayer.

The celebration of Easter starts with the end of Lent and the arrival of Palm Sunday. In Poland, Palm Sunday is called *Niedziela Męki Pańskiej (*the Sunday of the Lord's Passion*), Niedziela Wierzbowa (*Willow Sunday*) or Niedziela Kwietnia (*April Sunday). Lacking a convenient source of palms, the Poles substituted the spring greenery that would be in blossom in their areas. In Przezdziecko, the villagers cut willow branches to symbolize the palm branches covering Jesus's path to Jerusalem. The villagers placed the willow branches on the church floor to allow the priest and villagers to walk over them to the altar during the Palm Sunday procession. After the mass, the villagers took the branches home to place in their homes, barns, and fields to encourage good health, livestock production, and the protection of their homes. The family used branches to sprinkle the houses and outbuildings with holy water. They nailed willow branches to the main entries of the house and burnt them as incense to drive away evil spirits. Adam and the other villagers also fastened the branches to plows, tucked them into beehives, and put them under nests.

On Holy Thursday and Good Friday, Anna, her sisters, and the other girls in the village colored eggs. They did the coloring in secrecy from the boys and men. They called colored eggs *malowane* or *malowanki* when it was a single color. If they painted the egg with a design, it was called *kraszone* or *kraszanki*. *Pisanki* was the name used for a multi-colored egg that had intricate patterns. The origin of eggs as an Easter custom dates back to ancient times to celebrate the beginning of spring. In the 1800s, the Poles gave the elaborately decorated and ornamental *Pisanki* eggs as gifts during Polish courtships.

The family and the other villagers spent Good Friday fasting and praying in Church in memory of the Passion of Christ.

On Holy Saturday, Poles would go to the church with baskets full of eggs, sausages, and bread called the Easter Basket. The villagers would bring the Easter food to the church for the priests to bless. In small villages such as Przezdziecko, the Chmielewski family and the other villagers met the priest at a scheduled place and time to bless their Easter food. The priest made these trips to the small villages in the parish to avoid the risk of spoiling the food in the Easter Baskets.

On Easter Sunday, families would attend mass and then race home to meet their relatives for a festive breakfast. The fasting was over, and the blessed egg was the first food eaten. A slice of the egg was given to each family member to eat. Children believed they would get the sweets from the Easter Bunny, and sometimes, they looked for chocolate eggs hidden in the house. People wish one another a "Happy Easter" and enjoy visiting their friends and relatives on that day.

Easter Monday is called ***Śmigus-Dyngus*** or "Wet Monday." This was a celebration that people observed throughout Polish, Czech, Slovak, and Hungarian areas. On this day, the boys threw water over the girls. The girls returned the favor by throwing water on the boys the next day, but the boys often got soaked on Dyngus Monday. The boys took many girls to the nearby river or pond and were thrown into the water, thoroughly soaking them. The pretty girls were "watered" many times during the day. The girls often offered the boys a *pisanki* egg as a ransom and hoped this would save them from being soaked. They believed the eggs to be a magical charm that would bring good harvests, successful relationships, and healthy childbirths.

Other rituals followed the soakings, such as reciting verses and holding door-to-door processions. For example, in Przezdziecko, the boys would march through the villages, and one of them put on a bear costume with a bell on his head. The outfit was either a real bearskin or a bear-like suit of pea vines. The group would collect gifts for the bear by going door to door, and later, they would drown the bear in a nearby stream or pond. The Poles believed the bear had magical powers to prevent evil, provide for a good harvest, and help cure diseases.

The origins of the Dyngus celebration are uncertain, but it may date to pagan times, and its legend first appeared in writing as early as the 15th century. Some believe that water represents the spring rains needed for a successful harvest.

Summer – Feast of Corpus Christi

The Feast of Corpus Christi is a public holiday in Poland. The villagers in Przezdziecko celebrated it with pomp and ceremony when Anna lived there. It commemorated the Holy Eucharist. The feast was observed on the Thursday after Trinity Sunday, which usually fell in the latter part of May or early June.

In Przezdziecko, the villagers celebrated this holiday by observing three practices.

The first of these customs was the erection of four portable altars in a tent-like structure located away from the church. They decorated the inside of the tent with statues and holy pictures and made it resemble a small chapel.

The parishioners decorated altars with nine small wreaths. They made each wreath from a different herb – thyme (*macierzanka*), hazelwort (*kopytnik*), stonecrop (*rozchodnik*), lady's mantle (*nawrotek*), sundew (*rosiczka*), mint (*mieta*), rue (*ruta*), daisy (*strokroc)* and periwinkle (*barwinek*). The priest blessed the wreaths, which hung on the monstrance that held the Eucharist for a week. The blessing begged the Lord to accept the herbs' fragrance and bless those who submitted the wreaths.

The most important part of the Corpus Christi celebration was the procession. In their Sunday best clothes, the entire parish assembled in Andrzejewo to participate in the procession. The parish appointed an honor guard to lead the Blessed Sacrament at the head of the procession. Trade guild members followed this group, with town officials, religious organizations, individuals, and family groups. The people in the procession publicly proclaimed and reaffirmed their devotion to the Holy Eucharist. The march began by walking around the church, the grounds, and then the small temporary chapel. Finally, the congregation stopped at each of the small altars to pray and sing in adoration of the Eucharist. These devotions took place for eight days.

After the last devotion, the parishioners placed the birch branches among the growing field crops, believing they would protect the plants from hail. After the harvest, Adam and the other farmers of Przezdziecko took the first sheaves of grain from the field and placed them on a clean floor in the barn in the shape of a cross. They then laid one of the wreaths blessed at the Feast of Corpus Christi on top of the sheaves. Finally, all who helped with the harvest would make the sign of the cross, and the farmer would pray from St John's gospel. The parishioners hoped that this final ceremony would help protect the harvest from disease and troublesome pests such as mice and rats.

Fall – September weddings

The wedding ceremonies started in rural Poland in the fall after the villagers had finished harvesting the grain, completed all of the fieldwork, and milled the grain. The ceremonies continued through the fall and winter months until the spring fieldwork began.

Early Polish parents would arrange marriages for their children to protect their lands and find suitable husbands for their daughters. By the early 1900s, couples could choose their spouse, but the marriage process still included discussions with the family and constantly sought their approval.

In another custom, they probably used a *tarantowate* to help find a husband. Finally, fathers could announce the desire to marry off a daughter by painting white dots on the side of the home.

It was the custom in Poland for the male to approach the family for their daughter's hand in marriage. He has usually accompanied the *swat,* who did all of the talking. The initial meetings were called *wypytanie* in the Przezdziecko area, and their purpose was to determine if the family would welcome the man's proposal. The girl could veto continuing the discussions if she did not want to marry the man. If the family refused the man's proposal, it was done indirectly, not to insult him. If, however, they accepted it, it caused a grand celebration. The engagement was called *zaręczyny,* and the families considered it as binding as the marriage. The public ceremony included tying together the hands of the bride and groom on the night of the engagement. The following day, the couple went to the priest to place the marriage banns. The engagement lasted three weeks as the priests read the banns during a parish church mass.

The wedding ceremony was at the bride's parish church, and the celebration was festive with music and dancing that lasted at least two days.

The wedding day sometimes began with the musicians going to the groom's home and playing some sad tunes for him. The groom would receive his parents' blessing and then follow the musicians to the bride's home.

However, the musicians would be at the bride's home playing festive tunes in some areas as the bride's friends and attendants gathered around her. The bride's friends helped by arranging her dress, hair, and veil. Sometimes, the older women joined in and began chanting traditional wedding songs, admonishing the bride about her duties.

After the groom arrived, the bridal couple knelt before the bride's parents, sprinkled the couple with holy water, and blessed them. After the blessing, the bride would receive her symbolic farewell from her parents and relatives. After the farewell speeches, the wedding party lined up for the march to the church. The musicians played for them as they left. During all this time, tears flowed freely.

The couple used one of the family carts to ride to the church. As they got onto the cart, they were showered with grains of oats and sprinkled with holy water. Then, the decorated cart, the horses, and the musicians followed the wedding party in the festive procession to the church.

The Polish villagers watch some traditions or superstitions on the wedding day.

One involved the candles on the altar during the ceremony. If a candle went out on the bride's side of the altar, she might die early. If the candle went out on the groom's side, he might die soon.

If the bride cried, she would have good luck, or the bride and groom would be unlucky if the day were rainy.

The musicians met at the wedding party in front of the house upon returning from the church.

Here, the bride's mother observed another tradition when she offered the young pair bread, salt, and wine. The parents hoped their children would never be hungry by providing bread. The salt reminded the couple that they might experience difficult times and must learn to cope with life's struggles. The parents wished the couple a happy life with good health and never to be thirsty by offering them wine.

The parents then kissed the newly married couple as a sign of welcome, unity, and love.

The family then brought out the wedding breakfast, which was as large as a dinner, regarding the quality and amount of food served. Next, the musicians began playing, and the guests heard beautiful songs throughout the feast. Finally, a master of ceremonies or *starosta* gave the bridal pair sincerely and then mocking advice.

Dancing began with the bride and groom. The bride had to dance with every male guest and was probably very tired when the dancing was interrupted by supper. Once everyone ate, the dancing resumed for the rest of the evening. The wedding guests took up a collection for the bride and groom instead of presenting gifts. This gift of money was to help pay the cost of the wedding and leave a comfortable nest egg.

Toward midnight on the second day of the wedding, the traditional capping ceremony began. The bride sat in the middle of the room with the guests standing in a large circle around her. One of the matrons took off the bride's veil. The custom merely removed the elaborate coiffure, a fancy headdress in earlier times.

After the unveiling, everyone sat down for the midnight supper. The guests resumed dancing as soon as the supper was over and continued with undiminished vigor until morning. Then, sleep for a few hours, dance, and feast for the following days. A Polish wedding was considered a real party.

What memories do you have of the holidays?
What do you remember about the holidays and your parents and grandparents?

The meaning of a holiday comes from a custom, practice, or tradition handed down by someone who has long since died but still holds a warm place in our hearts.

Write down your memories. Save them for your grandchildren and their children.

APPENDIX: REASONS TO EMIGRATE

Why did our Polish ancestors immigrate to America?

The first record of Polish people in America was in 1608. These were three Polish craftsmen hired by the London Company to make glass, pitch, and potash burners for the Jamestown settlement in Virginia. More Poles landed in 1619 to reinforce the manufacture of pitch and begin production of tar and resin used to repair ships.

The first significant series of events that affected the massive Polish immigration were the three partitions of Poland that occurred between 1772 and 1795. However, the Partitions and takeover by Russia, Austria, or Prussia did not cause Poles to leave. The reasons for emigration were complicated, but Poland's partitioning set in motion some of the factors that caused conditions to deteriorate in Poland and made the decision to leave easier. Throughout the partitions, political and cultural repression of the Polish nation led to some uprisings against the Russian, Prussian, and Austrian governments. Although the rulers of partitioned Poland were initially tolerant, their treatment of the Poles changed drastically after the series of uprisings in the 1800s. They added stricter laws and higher taxes. Prussia and Russia took additional steps and enacted laws to wipe out all traces of Polish culture. The uprisings also caused investors to shy away from industrial development in Poland. By the end of the 1800s, European economic problems and a lack of industrial development in Poland caused many people to live in poverty.

The waves of Polish immigration began in the 1850s. The severe economic problems faced by Polish peasants during the 1800s and early 1900s were why they began leaving. The Polish peasants gained their freedom in the early 1800s and were free to leave the land. However, granting the peasants freedom also negated the landowners' obligations to care for them. This act put many in survival mode. Foreign investors were reluctant to supply the money needed to build the factories in Poland due to their fears of more unrest and uprisings occurring. The lack of industrial development fueled widespread unemployment and poverty. Overcrowding prevented many sons of farmers from owning land. These were the major problems in all three partitions, as Prussia, Russia, and Austria neglected their Polish lands.

Polish peasants' emigration started in the 1850s when Poles left Silesia to settle near Panna Maria in Texas, Parisville in Michigan, and Portage County, Wisconsin. Panna Maria is considered the earliest Polish settlement in the United States. The Poles who immigrated to Texas left Upper Silesia from Opole, Strzelecki, Tossed-Gliwice, Lubliniec, and Olesno. They followed Father Leopold Moczygemba to land east of San Antonio, Texas, where they established the town of Panna Maria. Their documented history indicated they left for numerous reasons. One reason was the harsh poverty that existed in Silesia. Another was the social discrimination they suffered at their Prussian rulers' hands. They suffered through the reoccurring epidemics of cholera. They also had to pay high taxes, and then there was the conscription of their young men into the military.

Many Polish peasants began emigrating from the other Prussian areas in the late 1860s when the German Empire started its attempt to Germanize all of its non-German lands. The Kulturkampf Laws were enacted in 1871 to accelerate their policy further and eliminate the Polish culture in Prussian control of Polish lands. The German language became the official language, and the German authorities tried to suppress the use of the Polish language. The Germans closed the Polish-speaking schools and Polish-language newspapers. Traditional Polish songs and Polish dances were forbidden. In 1886, the Prussian Colonization Policy forced Poles to sell their lands to Germans recruited to re-settle in these new "German" lands. Large landowners received government support to improve farming methods, leading to higher production. Modern techniques also required fewer farm workers. Work for the Polish day laborer became rare because employers favored Germans when hiring. These policies forced the Polish farmers to emigrate because they could not feed their families from the meager wages of the day-laborer. Passenger lists from this period (1869 to 1899) indicate whole families left Polish Germany to settle in the cities and farms of America. Records show that over 400,000 Poles from German-controlled Poland emigrated between 1869 to 1899.

Another uprising occurred in the Russian partition in 1863. The nobility led the rebels, and the peasants supported them. The Poles tried again in 1864, but again, Russian forces defeated them. This defeat resulted in over 10,000 Poles emigrating, but many conquered Poles could not escape. The Russian military killed thousands of Poles and deported about 38,000 to Siberia.

The 1863 Polish uprising against the Tsar fueled the Russian ruler's decision to implement a harsh Russification policy. The new laws included the imposition of the Russian language, the forced conversion to the Orthodox Catholic religion, and the levy of heavy taxes. It also imposed the mandatory use of the Russian language on all official documents. The religious and cultural persecution and the petty treatment of the Poles by their Russian administrators caused a rise in Polish nationalism.

The lack of jobs available for the growing population of laborers Poles in the Russian regions magnified the economic problems endured by the people. Improved farm methods caused farmworkers to disappear, and the number of factory jobs was not growing. Russia had supported industrial development in their Polish lands in the early 1800s, but the Russian government began moving factories from Poland to Russian lands after the 1863 uprising. In addition, the Tsar established the Peasant Bank in 1883 to help eligible peasants buy farmland and satisfy their hunger for land. Although owning land discouraged some emigration, the Russification policies negated much of this effect, and migration grew. Russia also encouraged Polish laborers to move to industrial centers in Russia, such as Siberia.

Inheritance laws were another factor that caused emigration. The rules dictated that only the oldest son could receive the land, forcing many young men and women to leave Poland in the late 1880s and early 1900s. If the family-owned property, younger sons could not inherit the property and had no prospects of earning a living in rural areas. The large old estates were divided many times when each generation of nobles died. By the late 1700s, the inheriting generations subdivided the large estates into smaller farms. At that time, authorities changed the inheritance laws to allow only the oldest son to inherit the land. All other children had to find other means to support themselves and their families. Daughters had to find husbands with land, and sons had to find jobs. With the low level of industrial development in the northeast portion of Poland, non-farming jobs were rare, and emigration was the primary option.

The Poles were allowed to practice their Catholic faith in the Austrian area. However, the period is known as the "Galician Misery," which began about 1880. Farmers in the Austrian-controlled Polish regions saw their lives sink into poverty. Small farmers lost their farms to the more wealthy nobles and their means of supporting their families. Peasant farmers also lost their farms to nobles as mechanization made large farms more economical. Unfortunately, there were no large industrial cities where these farmers could find work. Therefore, they were forced to emigrate.

Another primary reason some Poles immigrated was due to fears of military conscription. Military service was mandatory for all three of Poland's foreign rulers, and the foreign officers assigned the Polish conscripts into segregated units. As a result, the Polish regiments were always the first sent into the battle and suffered the most massive losses compared to the other groups. For example, in the Russian Army, seventy-five percent of the Polish conscripts died in fighting during the 1800s.

The emigration of the Polish peasants in the Russian and Austrian partitions began in earnest in the 1880s. Most were the younger sons of Polish farmers who had no hope of owning land. With the lack of industrialization in Poland, owning property was the key to economic stability. If the family owned land, they could not subdivide the farm if the father died. The inheritance laws gave the properties to only one son, usually the oldest. The other sons found it challenging to find work because there were few jobs outside the family farm due to the lack of industrialization in these areas. If there were large manor farms in the area, the introduction of farm machinery replaced many farm laborers. It reduced the number of jobs available, and the number of young workers increased.

With these conditions and a lack of opportunities in rural Poland, the possibilities offered by emigrating to the United States became an attractive but scary alternative. But unfortunately, their chances to own a farm were zero for most, and emigration also provided a quick way out of the looming decade of serving in the Imperial armies.

Letters from earlier emigrants fueled thoughts by the Polish peasants to leave their poverty and find a new land with unlimited opportunities. Advertisements that the shipping companies circulated also increased ideas about the possibilities in America.

Sons who could not inherit land could not earn a living in their villages. They had to leave. Fathers had to find the "right husband" for their daughters or ship them to America. In America, these young Polish girls worked as servants or in the factories until they found a husband.

Passenger manifests indicate that most Polish immigrants from the Russian and Austrian partitions were single men and women. However, I did see some married Polish couples listed on the passenger manifests. In most instances, the husband left first to find work and a place to live. Then, once he earned the cost of the passage, he sent for his wife. Some couples had just married and seemingly agreed to a safe marriage in Poland instead of searching for a suitable spouse in America. Couples with children also emigrated from the Russian and Austrian partitions, although this happened more often from the Prussian area.

Another type of Polish emigrant left to earn money and then returned to buy farmland for themselves. Many of the men in this group emigrated, intending to return, but some found it hard to abandon their new land once they saw how much better their life was. However, almost a third of Polish immigrants returned to Poland after living in the United States for a few years.

Although many Poles returned to their homeland, most Polish immigrants stayed in America to make a better life.

In the last half of the 1800s and the early 1900s, historians divide the forces motivating the Poles to leave their homeland into "Push" and "Pull" factors.

Push factors were forces that drove them out of their home countries, such as:
- poverty
- a shortage of land
- the military draft
- political or cultural repression
- religious discrimination

Pull factors were:
- the promise of jobs in the new lands
- cheap farmland in America and Canada
- Introduction of low-cost Steerage passage
- the magnetic pull of "chain migration."

In the 1860s, cultural and religious persecution of the Poles by the Prussian and Russian monarchs became a significant factor in the migration of the Poles.

In the Prussian area:
- Poles were not allowed to speak Polish in public.
- Laws required all business to be conducted in German.
- Polish-speaking schools were closed, and schools taught the children in German.
- Poles were not allowed to print Polish newspapers,
- They were not allowed to perform traditional Polish dances or sing the Polish songs that they loved
- Government officials closed Catholic churches.
- Poles were forced to sell their lands, and Germans purchased farms at bargain prices.

In the Russian area:
- The Polish people in the Russian partition also suffered due to the Russian Tsar's Russification policy, which included the imposition of the Russian language, the conversion to the Orthodox Catholic religion, and the levy of heavy taxes.
- There was a mandatory 5 to 6 years of military service.
- Their Russian administrators' petty treatment of the Poles caused a rise in Polish nationalism.

In the Austrian area:
- The Poles were allowed to practice their Catholic faith, but most of the lower-class poverty led to high levels of immigration.

These factors added to the unrest among the Polish people and their desire to emigrate for a better life.

Immigration patterns of the Poles shifted drastically after World

War I. The re-formation of the Polish state into the Second Polish Republic drew an estimated 10,000 Poles to return to their ancestral homes. However, Poland was reborn and faced the daunting rebuilding of an extensively damaged country during World War I. The forming of a new Poland was also challenged by the differences in the Poles' political views in the three partitions. Immigration to the United States resumed, but the rate was lower.

Another change that affected Polish immigration was the introduction of quotas by U.S. immigration officials for each ethnic group of immigrants beginning in 1921. The first law passed by the United States Congress that set quotas defined levels based on 3 percent of the population by country of origin based on the 1910 U.S. Census. However, in 1924, that percentage was lowered to 2 percent of the people by country of origin based on the 1890 Census. Since the number of immigrants arriving from Poland peaked during the early 1900s, using the 1910 census data would have been much fairer than the data from the 1890 census. Before 1890, immigration from Poland started to accelerate, and using the 1890 data would understate the percentage of the population who came from Poland. Basing the quota on the 1890 census data allowed only 5000 Poles to enter the United States per year after 1924. The quota calculation changed again in 1927, and the 1920 census data became the basis for calculating quota levels.

Fear of war in Europe grew in the 1930s, causing many Polish children born in the United States to leave their parents in Poland and return to the United States. My grandparents had one nephew immigrate to the United States in 1938, and another returned in 1939. Both men had been born in the U.S. before their parents returned to Poland after World War I. One enlisted and served in the U.S. Army during World War II. I do not have the statistics, but passenger manifests indicate many American-born sons and daughters of repatriated Polish immigrants returned to the U.S. before World War II. After the war ended and a Communist government took control of Poland, many more Polish children returned to the land where they were born.

Why did your Ancestors Immigrate?

- Remember that each immigrant has a unique story
- Our challenge is to dig out as many details as possible with our research.
- Some of the above reasons may fit the situations your ancestors left in Poland, and you should include them in your family history narrative.
- Then, include family oral history, which may add other facts and insights. Finally, remember what your ancestors passed down, as the reason they left was the last straw that pushed them to make a decision.

GLOSSARY

POLISH TERMS

akta małżenstw	marriage records
akta urodzin	birth records
akta zgonów	death records
babka	grandmother
bałtycki	Baltic
brat	brother
bratanek	nephew
bratanica	niece
chałupnik, chałupnikow	cottager, poor peasant, serf, of serfs
chłop	peasant, country fellow
choroba	disease
chrzestna, chrzestny	godparent(s)
córka	daughter
dobra	estate
dziadek	belongs to the grandfather
dziadka	of grandfather
dziadunio	grandfather
dziedzic	Heir, country gentleman
dzwonki za konajacych	Ringing of the bells for the dying
emigracja	emigration
folwark	manor farm
gromica	the candle that was blessed at the Feast of Purification
grunt	land, property
gubernia	Russian province
Gwiazdory	A caroling group dressed as the three Wisemen
imię (imiona)	given name(s)
imigracja	immigration

Koszula śmiertelna.	Death shirt
kukielki	Ritual bread for christening
las	forest, woods

Łowcy gulasz	Hunter's stew is made with sauerkraut and meat.
małżonka	wife
Mazovia	a historical region in mid-north-eastern Poland
mielony kotlet	Fried minced meat roll
Mizeria	Salad made with cucumbers in sour cream and dill
najmlodszy	youngest
najstarszy	oldest, eldest
narodzony	born
nowe laki	ritual bread for New Year's celebration
Okolica szlachecka	a noble-owned settlement
opłata	the poor peasant, crofter, gardener
opłatek	Christmas wafer
opuchlizna	father
parafia	parish
parobek	Farm worker
Pisanki	Decorated eggs are usually for Easter.
r. (Roku)	in the year
robotnik	worker
Schabowy kotlet	Breaded pork tenderloin
siostra	sister
Słownik Geograficzny Krolestwa Polskiego	The Geographical Dictionary of the Kingdom of Poland is a gazetteer for Polish villagers.
służący	servant
Surówka warzywna	Salad made with sauerkraut, apples, carrots, and onion
swaty	Using go-betweens to arrange a

	marriage
swięty	holy
szlachecki (szlachety)	noble
szlachta	nobility
szopka	crib or manger

tarantowate	Dotting the sides of homes with white paint to announce the desire of a father to marry off a daughter
urodzony	born, wellborn (noble)
wydany	military
zupa mleczna	breakfast food of cereal grain and milk

ENGLISH TERMS

Chain Immigration	Immigration to a specific place due to following someone who is known to the immigrant
Congress of Poland (1815-1919)	A portion of Poland under Russian control was created in 1815 by the Congress of Vienna, which granted the Polish nobles in that area a degree of autonomy.
Declaration for Citizenship	First step in the naturalization process for U.S. citizenship
hectares	0.4047 acres
Kingdom of Poland (1815-1919)	A portion of Poland under Russian control was created in 1815 by the Congress of Vienna, which granted the Polish nobles in that area a degree of autonomy.
London Company	A group of English investors whom King James I of England chartered to establish colonial settlements in North America
naturalization petition	The second step in the naturalization process, since 1906, includes many details identifying the applicant.
Packard Motor Car Company	Produced automobiles in Detroit, Michigan, starting in 1899, and later by the Studebaker-Packard Corporation of South Bend, Indiana, until 1958
partible inheritances	The system of inheritance that distributes the estate of the deceased to all heirs
Polish partitions	A series of three annexations of Polish lands between 1772 and 1795 resulted in the Russian Empire, the Kingdom of Prussia, and Habsburg Austria taking control of all Polish territory.
primogeniture	the system of inheritance by the eldest son
Russification policy	Forced cultural assimilation of the Polish people that included the mandatory use of the Russian language and conversion to the Russian Orthodox Church

INDEX

ABOUT THE AUTHOR

Steve Szabados is a genealogy author and lecturer. He has been researching his ancestors since 2000 and has traced them back to the 1600s in Virginia and New England, and to the 1730s in Poland, Germany, Bohemia, Hungary, Slovakia, and Slovenia. He has given numerous presentations to genealogical groups and libraries in Illinois, Indiana, Michigan, Missouri, Pennsylvania, and Wisconsin. His mission is to share his passion for Family History with as many people as possible. He is a member of the Northwest Suburban Genealogy Society and the Illinois State Genealogical Society. He is a former board member of the Polish Genealogical Society of America and a volunteer in genealogy at the Arlington Heights Memorial Library. Steve is also a genealogy columnist for the Polish American Journal.

Books by Steve

Finding Grandma's European Ancestors: Revised 2016
Want to find your European roots? This book gives you easy steps to find where your ancestors left and tips for locating their European records. Most European countries are covered.
Print book

Irish Immigration to America
This is a fantastic resource and a must-have when writing your Irish family history. When did your Irish ancestors immigrate, where did they leave, why did they leave, and how did they get here? Many factors drove Irish immigration, and the Great Potato Famine only magnified the main causes. The author hopes you find the answer to some of these questions. This book will provide insight into answering some of these questions.
Print book and eBook

German Immigration to America
Why did your German ancestors immigrate, when they left, where they left, and how did they get here? This book is a fantastic resource that may help you find answers to these questions and insights about your ancestors' immigration.
Print book and eBook

Find Your Czech and Slovak Ancestors
This book is an excellent source for finding your ancestors' Czech and Slovak records. The book outlines a simple process to identify where your ancestors were born and where to find their European records.
Print book

Czech and Slovak Immigration to America: When, Where, Why, and How

When did your Czech or Slovak ancestors immigrate, where did they leave, why they left, and how they got here? This book is a wonderful resource. The author hopes you find the answer to some of these questions in this book. This book discusses the history of their homeland and gives some insights into possible answers to the questions about your ancestors' immigration.
Print book and eBook

Polish Genealogy: Four Steps to Success

This book gives the researcher the tools needed to research their Polish ancestors and find possible answers to the origins of their Polish heritage. The book outlines a simple process to identify where your ancestors were born and where to find their Polish records.
Print book

Polish Immigration to America: When, Where, Why, and How

When did your Polish ancestors immigrate, where did they leave, why they left, and how did they get here? These are questions we all hope to find the answers. This book discusses the history of Poland and gives some insights into possible answers to the questions about your ancestors' immigration.
Print book and eBook

My Polish Grandmother: from Tragedy in Poland to her Rose Garden in America

The story of Anna's life is different from many stories of immigrants because it is told from a woman's perspective. She suffered through tragedies in her life in Poland but found the strength to build a new life in the U. S.
Print book and eBook

Memories of Dziadka
This book is about the life of a Polish immigrant – his early life in Poland, his travel to America, and his life in Illinois. I also try to describe why his simple life was essential to us.
Print book and eBook

Hints for Translating Polish Genealogical Records
A quick reference guide to help the researcher translate the Polish genealogical records of their ancestors.
eBook

DNA and Genealogy Research
DNA testing has become a popular topic with genealogists, but many times, the results are confusing. It is a powerful tool, but I am one of the many who find it challenging to educate myself on the science of DNA. I did not want to become a genetic scientist; I just wanted to work on my family history. The book explains my methods using non-scientific terms and does not discuss Chromosome browsers, haplogroups, or SNPs. I had a brick wall and used my genealogical skills and traditional sources with my DNA results to solve the mystery.
Print book and eBook

Write Your Family History: Easy Steps to Organize, Save and Share
Writing a family history can seem to be a very challenging project for many people. However, organizing your research into a format your family reads easily is a must. The methods discussed in this book will show the reader a simple format that will make this task much easier.
Print book and eBook

Basic Genealogy: Saving Your Family History
Find your roots! Start your search now. This book reviews a process that will help everyone start their research, giving hints that will make your research successful.
Print book and eBook

Basic Genealogy and Beyond Easy steps to find your Family History and tips to break down Brick Walls
This book goes beyond the great tips I covered in "Basic Genealogy." It gives many additional methods and sources to find more information to help create an excellent family history of your ancestors. In addition, my new book includes new material that covers search tips, organization, an outline of steps to find where your European immigrants left, and the basics of using DNA testing in genealogy.
Print book and eBook

Deciphering the 1790-1840 U.S. Census Records: Two case studies
Census records are a snapshot of your family, and finding all of these records is a critical task in researching your family history. This book reviews two case studies that will give you hints on how to decipher the early U.S. census, which is challenging to use because they list only the head of the household.
eBook

Quick Reference to U.S. Census Records: a snapshot of the past
Census records were a snapshot of your family when the census was taken. As a result, the document contains a wealth of information you can include in a family history. This book explains the information in the census records and how they can be used in your family histories. The book also points to where these records can be found and consists of some search tips.
eBook